GERMAN ARMY UNIFORMS
of WORLD WAR II
in COLOUR PHOTOGRAPHS

GERMAN ARMY UNIFORMS of WORLD WAR II in COLOUR PHOTOGRAPHS

Wade Krawczyk

Windrow & Greene

© Wade Krawczyk 1995

This edition published in
Great Britain 1995 by
Windrow & Greene Ltd.
5 Gerrard Street
London W1V 7LJ

Designed by Tony Stocks, TS Graphics
Printed and bound in Spain

A CIP catalogue record for this book
is available from the British Library

ISBN 1-85915-052-7

Introduction

When I began collecting German militaria some twenty years ago, detailed and authoritative reference material was in short supply. Like so many collectors, the first book I acquired was Brian L.Davis's *German Army Uniforms and Insignia 1933-1945*; and this remained the standard reference work for many years. More recently the available range of good books on the subject has broadened considerably, to the point where almost every aspect has been covered. However, at a militaria fair some years ago I saw (and narrowly missed buying) a book which made me realise what was missing. The book was from a European war museum, and showed their uniform collection posed by a live model and photographed in full colour. The impact of seeing the uniforms in colour, after years of poring over black and white pictures, was striking. While the careful study of period photographs obviously remains of central importance for the collector, the opportunity to compare them with colour pictures of surviving uniforms seems to me invaluable.

"Knowledge is power", and there can be few fields in which this is more true than the collecting of militaria - particularly given the wide range of counterfeit items, spawned by high demand and high prices, which lie in wait for the student of World War II German uniforms. Protection from fakes, reproductions and altered items comes not from a superior bank balance, but only from an intimate knowledge of what one is collecting. Research is not a chore, but a natural and satisfying aspect of the collecting experience. One should know what was worn, why it was worn, what it was made from and what it looks like. Ultimately, of course, there is no substitute for actually handling a wide range of original items; but for most collectors the practical starting point must be a carefully assembled reference library.

My hope is that by having the chance to study the different items in this collection "on the man" and in close-up colour photographs, the reader will benefit from increased familiarity with their appearance in use and with some of the wide range of detail differences which may be encountered. Whilst there might seem at a glance to be a fair degree of similarity between some of the pieces illustrated, a closer look will reveal that no two items are actually the same. And that is the beauty of collecting.

A brief note about nomenclature may be in order. I have tried to include the original German terms for the different items of uniform and equipment, categories of unit, etc.; but for ease of reading I have used common-sense English translations for most repetitions. The distinction between "enlisted men" and "NCOs" follows German military practice; the former term is used here for the junior ranks distinguished by badges of rank - if any - worn on the sleeve, the latter for more senior non-commissioned ranks distinguished by braid edging to the collar and shoulder straps. In common with most texts on uniform and insignia materials and colours, terms such as "silver", "gold", "silk", etc., should be taken here to mean "made from materials having the appearance of...".

Acknowledgements

While the majority of the items shown are from my personal collection, other people have contributed material, encouragement or both. Special thanks go to Peter Gronow, who sold me my first original uniform in 1975 and who has encouraged and educated me ever since; to this day he remains a good friend. I would also like to thank Mark Stevens, Peter Roberts, David Grimshaw and Steve Meiburg for contributing items for photography; the models, for their patience, and for their endurance under the heat of the lights; Martin Windrow, for his encouragement; and Alan Mowbray, for the MG42. Finally I must thank my parents, my brother, and my wife Melissa for putting up with my hobby for so long. Thanks to you all.

WK
Tallebudgera
Queensland
June 1995

Contents

(1) Infantry NCO, walking-out dress, Germany 1937-39

The parade dress tunic (*Waffenrock*) was introduced in June 1935 and presented a general appearance resembling the dress uniform of the old Imperial Army, incorporating traditional Prussian motifs. The tunic was designed without external pockets, and cut to fit closely. The wearer's branch of service was reflected by the display of *Waffenfarbe* - the system of colouring for uniform adornments. This was seen on the parade and walking-out dress as piping on the tunic, shoulder straps and trousers, and backing for the metallic thread *Litzen* - decorative "lace" bars - on collar and cuffs.

The primary use of this uniform was as the ceremonial parade dress, when it was worn with the steel helmet, marching boots and rifle belt order. Its secondary use was as the walking-out uniform for civil functions and off-duty formal wear, when it was worn with the service dress cap (*Schirmmütze*), shoes, and a highly polished issue belt. A privately purchased dress sabre was sometimes worn off duty by NCOs, suspended by a hanger from under the tunic.

The manufacture of these dress tunics was abolished at the outbreak of World War II; but in the pre-war Army any soldier had the right to purchase privately a tailor-made dress tunic, and it was usually NCOs who took advantage of this privilege. The tailored tunics exhibited a higher quality of materials and workmanship, with more fashionable features such as a higher and more pointed collar. The example illustrated, made by a Hannover tailor, is named to *Unteroffizier* Heins, 9th Company, 57th Infantry Regiment, and dated 20.4.1937; private purchase tunics usually have an embroidered tailor's label at the neck, and an owner's label in the pocket. This tunic is made of a fine grade, lightly ribbed twill material with a green satin-effect lining; the sleeves are lined with grey and white striped material. The *Waffenfarbe* piping is white, for the Infantry. One pocket was provided inside the left breast, and two hidden pockets behind the decorative rear flaps of the tunic skirt.

The insignia on this tunic are mostly of the regular issue quality, although some NCOs did purchase officer-quality *Litzen*. This soldier has, however, purchased an officer-quality hand-embroidered national emblem (*Hoheitszeichen*) - the eagle and swastika, worn on the right breast by all ranks of the German Army. The shoulder straps have rounded (rather than the earlier pointed) inner ends; on these tunics they are always of the sewn-in variety, having the outer end let into the shoulder seam. The unit number was normally embroidered in the centre of the strap with *Waffenfarbe* - coloured thread, but sometime in the late 1930s some units ordered that these be removed, as in this case. The 1.5cm silver *Tresse* braid which distinguished NCO ranks was applied to the collar and cuffs. This soldier wears on his left breast the DRL sports proficiency badge, pinned through sewn attachment loops.

The colour of the tunic is officially described as field-grey (*Feldgrau*), but field-green is probably a more appropriate description. The trousers were of a stone-grey (*Steingrau*) fabric, with *Waffenfarbe* piping down the outer seam. These trousers were of superior quality, with a wide cut, and usually had adjustment tabs at each hip. Occasionally the side pockets were false or sewn closed, for a better appearance.

The peaked service cap (*Schirmmütze*) was the formal headdress of the Army. Early caps had a "saucer"-shaped crown (*Tellerform*) which officially changed to a "saddle" shape (*Sattelform*) in 1935, although enlisted ranks' caps continued to be seen in the *Tellerform* for some time. The dark green band and field-grey crown were piped in *Waffenfarbe*; the front bore, on the band, the Army's oakleaf wreath with the cockade in national colours, and on the crown the national eagle. These badges were generally made of stamped white metal, though private purchase caps sometimes had woven wire insignia. The patent leather chinstrap was worn on all enlisted men's and NCOs' caps. The issue cap had a rust-brown linen lining, with a transparent celluloid sweatshield sewn inside the crown; as well as protecting the lining, the shield featured a small slot into which a name tag could be inserted. Enlisted men's caps encountered with manufacturers' trade markings on the sweatshield are private purchase items. The leather sweatband was intended to be the same colour as the lining and the underside of the peak, but is occasionally encountered in other shades.

The sword is a standard non-commissioned grade type, manufactured by the respected firm of WKC in Solingen. The hilt is of the "dove's-head" pattern with a nickel silver finish.

Left
The peaked service cap, Schirmmütze, for all enlisted ranks. This example retains the "Tellerform" or "saucer" shape, and is piped in the white Waffenfarbe identifying the Infantry branch of service.

Far left
The interior of this cap exhibits the proper matching peak, lining and sweatband. The underside of the sweatband is stamped "5/I.R.116", for 5th Company, 116th Infantry Regiment. Note that the top (rear) portion of the sweatshield is missing in this case; with use the brittle material could crack along the lines of stitch holes.

Left
The enlisted ranks' dress tunic, Waffenrock, its traditional cut and style recalling the Prussian military heritage. Note the contrast between the field-grey shade of the Waffenrock and the stone-grey of the uniform trousers worn with it.

Right
The insignia. The silver Tresse braid indicating non-commissioned rank (from Unteroffizier upwards) is applied to the top and front edges of the collar, rather than to the bottom and front as on the service tunic. The collar and Swedish cuffs are both faced with dark green "badge cloth", and are edged - like the front left hand panels - with 0.2cm piping in branch Waffenfarbe. This colour is also seen as the backing for the collar and cuff patches. Note in this case an officer-quality breast eagle, embroidered in silver wire on dark green backing; and the marksmanship lanyard, with the original 1936 style of plaque. The lanyard has two attached silver acorns, making this award the third grade.

Right
The lining of this tunic, named to Unteroffizier Heins of 9/I.R.57, displays many of the features found in privately purchased garments. There is a full lining; the sleeves are also fully lined, with a contrasting striped material. The tunic has a fabric internal waist belt allowing careful adjustment for fit. The woven tailor's label sewn in at the neck identifies Traugott Rahne of Hannover.

Below right
This private purchase NCO's sword, while of a standard pattern and fitted with a regulation sword knot, displays a non-regulation tradition badge - an enamelled shield in the colours of the Sudetenland.

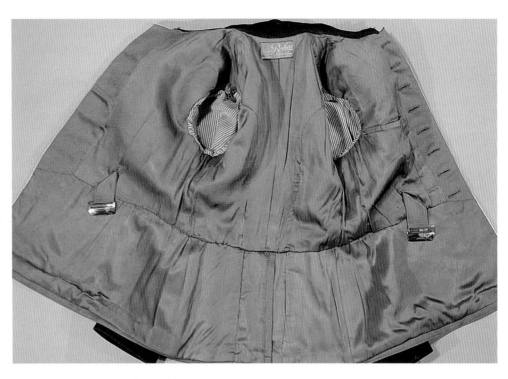

(2) Armoured Troops officer, parade dress, Germany 1937-39

When the armoured branch was created in 1934 the black "special purpose" uniform (*Sonderbekleidung der Panzertruppen*) was introduced specifically for wear when working or parading with the vehicle, and not as everyday dress. Soldiers of the *Panzer* arm also received the full scale of field-grey service uniform issue. For dismounted ceremonial the parade dress (*Paradeanzug*) was worn, as it was by all other branches of the Army.

The full dress uniform for officers was of traditional design, with the wearer's branch of service denoted by the coloured *Waffenfarbe* piping and badge backing. The tailoring of this pattern of dress was ordered to be discontinued after the outbreak of the war; however, those who already possessed the uniform were entitled to wear it as a walking-out dress or full dress at appropriate functions such as weddings and other formal events. Before the outbreak of war this *Grosser Gessellschaftanzug* was the official full dress for officers of all arms of service.

The parade tunic for officers was of the same basic design as that for enlisted ranks, though distinguished by the silver embroidered insignia and by appointments such as the aiguillette and the belt. This tailored example displays a high degree of quality and workmanship. The body is made from a fine field-grey tricot material, and has no external pockets. The front closure has eight silver pebbled-finish buttons, with two hooks and eyes at the collar. The collar and cuffs are faced with dark green badge cloth and edged, like the left front panel, with *Waffenfarbe* piping. The rear skirt has two piped ornamental pocket flaps with three buttons, the upper pair being slotted to act as belt supports. Inside the skirt, behind these decorative flaps, are a pair of small functional slash pockets. The lining of the body is of grey satin-finish material, and the sleeves are lined with pin-striped cotton. There is an internal pocket inside the left breast, and the usual internal waist belt to ensure a perfect fit. This particular tunic also has a sweat pad fitted in each armpit to prevent staining. The tailor's label at the neck reads "Karl Werner Meiningen".

The collar patches have richly embroidered double *Litzen* on a base of the Armoured Troops' rose-pink *Waffenfarbe* ; the patches on the Swedish cuffs are similar, but with single *Litzen* bearing buttons. The breast eagle, while hand-embroidered, is in this case mounted on mid-green backing of rather mediocre quality. The shoulder straps display the rank of *Major*, with rose-pink *Waffenfarbe* bases and bright silver plaited cords.

The M35 *Stahlhelm* was worn for parades; while most officers wore the issue steel helmet, some chose to purchase lightweight copies made of *Vulkanfiber* or aluminium, which were sold by most leading hatmakers. The riding breeches and kneeboots were worn with the dress tunic for ceremonial parades, being replaced for walking-out and off-duty formal occasions by straight trousers with *Waffenfarbe* seam piping and low shoes. The other appointments worn with this uniform were the full dress belt and aiguillette. The belt, introduced in July 1937, was of silver ribbed brocade with two horizontal dark green stripes; the circular stamped white metal buckle showed the *Wehrmachts-Adler* surrounded by an oakleaf wreath. The aiguillette, which

replaced the old *Reichsheer* pattern in June 1935, were purely decorative, and were worn with the parade and walking-out tunic by all officers and administrative officials with officer status. They comprised a pair of plaited silver cords with ornamental ferrules, and two straight cords; a buttonhole tab in the centre engaged with a button concealed under the right shoulder strap, and the free ends fastened to the second front tunic button.

The sabre was required wear for full dress parades, the officer's dress dagger not being permitted with the brocade dress belt. The sabre was worn suspended from a concealed internal cloth waist or shoulder belt, with a nickel clip which engaged a horizontal bar on the reverse of the scabbard.

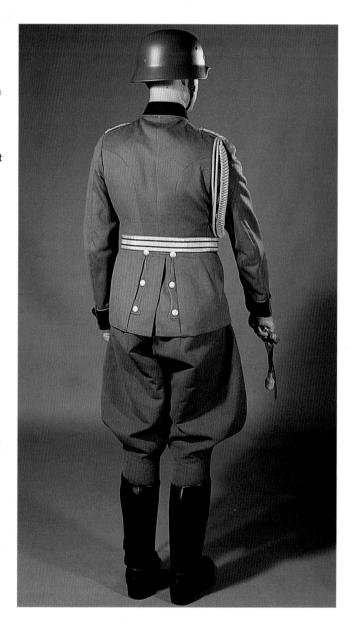

Far left
The M35 steel helmet (Stahlhelm) replaced the original Great War pattern introduced in 1916 and retained until 1935 (and even after that date, in some cases). Before the war all Army helmets displayed two insignia applied to the sides as transfers: the tricolour national shield on the right side, and the Wehrmachts-Adler, in silver-grey on a black shield, on the left.

Above right
The M31 leather helmet lining, adjustable for size by a drawstring, was mounted on a slightly padded aluminium band which was itself attached to the helmet with three split pins; note the attachments for the chinstrap.

Left
The full dress tunic. Note the thread loops worked high and low on the left breast; very commonly seen on all types of tunic, these allowed the wear of pin-back medal ribbon bars and award badges without piercing the tunic itself.

Right
All insignia are embroidered in bright silver metallic thread, the Litzen and shoulder straps being backed with the Panzer arm's rose-pink Waffenfarbe. Note the method of wearing the dress aiguillette; thesewere identical for all ranks (below general officers) and all branches of service.

Right
The dress belt usually came in a circular cardboard container, often together with the aiguillette; this example has a woven maker's tag at the rear for "Franze Sprangemacher Oldenburg". The buckle is flanked by a pair of brocade loops and a pair of rectangular keepers, one of which acted as a catch for the hook behind the buckle. The belt was required to be completely backed with cloth, to prevent slipping.

Above
This sabre is fairly typical of the many designs available from a wide variety of makers. The eagle crossguard and the lion's-head pommel (here with red glass "ruby" eyes) are a feature of this model made by the respected Solingen firm of Eikhorn, whose name and squirrel trademark it bears.

(3) Infantry officer, white summer tunic, Germany 1938-39

The "new style white tunic" was an item of dress only available to officer ranks. It was introduced in July 1937 to replace the *Reichsheer* pattern of summer tunic, orders for wear stating that it could be worn only between 1 April and 30 September each year. The uniform could be worn as a walking-out dress, for mess functions, at civil gatherings and for sports events.

The tunic was constructed from a white linen material and displayed the shoulder straps and breast eagle, but regulations forbade the use of collar patches. All of the insignia and buttons could be removed to allow the garment to be laundered conveniently. The tunic was worn with the piped dress trousers and shoes or with riding breeches and kneeboots; no matching white trousers existed. The peaked service cap was worn; medals and awards were displayed, as was the officer's dress dagger at some formal functions. There was no designated wearing-out period and the white tunic was retained by many officers well into the war years. It was not worn in the field.

The white tunic (*Weisser Rock für Offiziere, neuerer Vorschrift*) was cut to the same pattern as the officer's service tunic, and the material used could vary from a "waffle" pattern cotton to a slightly ribbed twill. There were four patch pockets with box pleats, the buttoned flaps cut to a three-point scalloped shape. The eight buttons down the front closure were the standard 19mm pebbled-finish type in bright silver, attached to the tunic with split pins which allowed their easy removal. The rear of the tunic was cut in a traditional fashion, with the rear seams arching down from the shoulder seam to the small of the back, where two removable buttons were attached. The body of the tunic was cut to fit closely, especially at the waist; there was no lining. The collar was a pointed fall type (unlike the "old style" *Reichsheer* white tunic, which had a straight standing collar).

The breast eagle worn with this tunic was stamped in a silver-coloured light metal, and attached by a horizontal pin and hook which passed through thread loops above the right pocket. Some examples also had a vertical hook behind the swastika to further secure the badge. The shoulder straps had a small stiff fabric bar sewn to their outer ends, projecting in a T-shape; they were inserted through an opening in the shoulder seam, the bar preventing their slipping out, and buttoned down at the inner end in the usual way. The straps seen here are of the pre-war pattern, with bright silver cord; they display the single gold star identifying the rank of *Oberleutnant*, and underlay in the white *Waffenfarbe* of the Infantry. The aiguillette worn here denotes the appointment of unit adjutant.

The cap is the 1935 pattern officer's *Schirmmütze*; the previous model had had a field-grey band. The crown was manu-factured in a range of materials, quality varying according to cost. They will be found in fabrics such as serge, tricot, and the woollen material illustrated, which was known as *Eskimo*; many differing shades of field-grey and field-green will also be encountered by collectors. The band is of dark green badge cloth, and the *Waffenfarbe* piping here is Infantry white. The peak is made from a vulcanised fibre (*Vulkanfiber*) which is lacquered black. The lining of this cap is made of a bronze-coloured silk, with the sweatshield imprinted with the

manufacturer's trademark - in this case "Erel" of Berlin, regarded as one of the best cap-makers. The sweatband is made from thin beige leather with a ribbon finishing bow at the rear seam. The doubled silver (aluminium) bullion chin cords are secured by two 12mm pebbled-finish buttons; these cords were always worn above the peak. The national eagle is stamped from a silvered light metal; the wreath and national cockade are of woven bullion thread - a common combination of materials. The badge worn here between these national and Army insignia is the so-called Brunswick pattern death's-head, a tradition badge worn by all ranks of 17.Infanterie-Regiment.

The dress trousers worn here are in stone-grey with white *Waffenfarbe* outer seam piping. They have straight-cut legs, with a slash pocket at either hip and one at the right rear.

The officer's dress dagger was approved in May 1935 and was retained until forbidden for wear after September 1944. The grips will be encountered in orange-yellow, white, and occasionally ivory, which was a private purchase option.

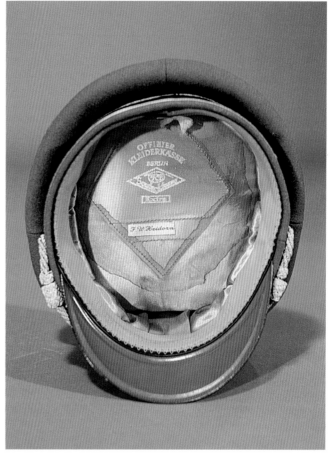

Above
This Schirmmütze was the standard officer's peaked service cap of the war years. The piping of the band and crown was coloured according to the branch of service. The Totenkopf tradition badge worn on this example was a privilege of the 17th Infantry Regiment, recalling the old 92nd Brunswick Infantry Regiment of Imperial days, which itself traced its lineage - and the death's-head badge - to the "Black Brunswickers" of the Napoleonic Wars.

Above right
This high quality cap lining features the "Erel" trademark of a famous Berlin maker printed on the sweatshield. Note the owner's name-tag in the slot formed by the sweatshield stitching.

Right
The pattern of the "new style white tunic for officers" is outwardly almost identical to that of the field-grey officer's service tunic, though unlined and cut to a tight fit.

Opposite bottom left
Details of the tunic insignia: note pin-on metal breast eagle and detachable shoulder straps. The wearing of collar patches on this tunic was forbidden, though some general officers exercised their right to do so. Note the method of wearing the unit adjutant's aiguillette (Adjutant-schnüre), which differs in design and method of attachment from the previously illustrated officer's parade aiguillette (Achselbänder).

Opposite top
The interior of the white summer tunic, which is completely unlined. Note inside the shoulder seams the exposed retaining crossbars of field-grey cloth sewn beneath the outer ends of the shoulder straps; and the split rings which secure the detachable buttons.

Opposite bottom right
The Army officer's dress dagger was worn suspended by the braid-faced cloth hangers from an internal belt, with the service dress or the dress uniform. Note the method of tying the silver cord dagger knot (Portepee).

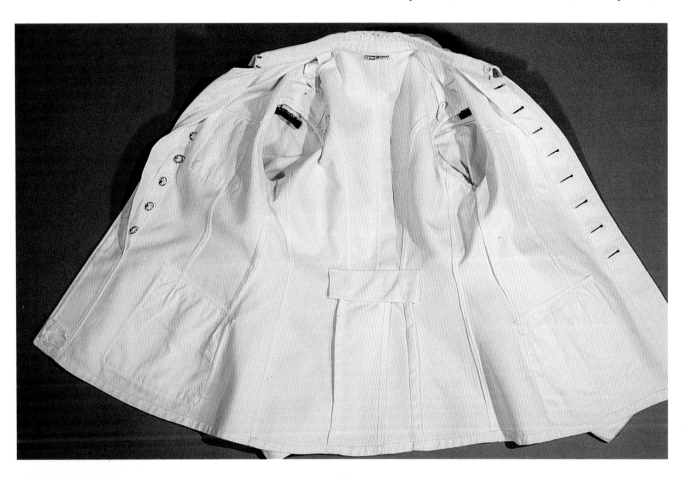

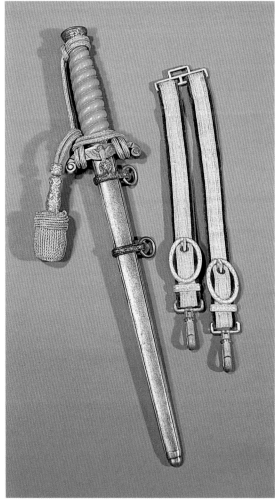

(4) Infantry enlisted man, fatigue dress, Germany 1934-40

The fatigue or drill uniform (*Drillichanzug*) was issued to all soldiers on joining the Army. Introduced in April 1933, it consisted of a cream or off-white jacket and trousers, and was worn for some field exercises, drill training, work details, weapons instruction and cleaning, vehicle maintenance, or any other duty which might soil or damage the service dress. The light colour naturally showed up any stains or wear very noticeably, and during the 1930s trials were conducted with a field-grey material, for the sake of maintaining a better appearance. However, these were discontinued in April 1938; and with the outbreak of World War II the colour was changed to reed-green in 1940. Once this more practical colour had been adopted the fatigue uniform began to find favour among front line troops as an improvised hot weather field service dress. The white uniform jacket carried only sleeve rank insignia for enlisted grades, with no breast eagle, collar patches or shoulder straps. However, with the appearance of the reed-green jacket in the field all or some of these insignia were to be seen attached despite being contrary to regulations. In this mode it became the predecessor of the reed-green service uniform (see section 16).

The fatigue uniform was cut from a hard-wearing cotton drill material with a "herringbone" weave. The natural off-white colour was soon corrupted by wear and frequent washing, and these garments will be encountered in a variety of shades. The jacket was single-breasted, of a generous cut, with five buttons down the front closure; these were detachable, being secured by S-shaped split rings which were hidden behind the inside lining. There was an open patch pocket at each hip. The only insignia worn on this jacket were a series of rank badges for junior enlisted grades, embroidered in light grey on an off-white drill backing and sewn to the upper left sleeve.

The drill trousers were made of the same material and were of a loose cut with straight legs. The waist was cut high at the back, with a horizontal adjustment tab and buckle. A slash pocket was provided at each hip, as well as a small fob pocket and chain loop at the right groin. Suspender (braces) buttons, and the five fly buttons, were of the metal dish-shaped type.

The marching boots (*Marschstiefel*) were one of the most traditional and recognisable pieces of the German soldier's uniform. Leather and workmanship were both of high quality. The sole had between 35 and 45 hobnails, depending on size, with an iron "horseshoe" around the outer rim of the heel and an iron "scuff plate" at the toe.

This soldier, wearing fatigue uniform with the M34 field cap ("*Schiffschen*" or "little ship", so called from its shape), is pictured cleaning the bore of his 7.92mm Karabiner 98k rifle with the chain "pull-through"; this bolt-action weapon was introduced in 1934 and remained standard issue throughout the wartime German armed forces. (It was little changed from its predecessors in the classic series of Mauser rifles stretching back into the 19th century, however, and the magazine still held only five rounds.) The soldier wears belt equipment for light training duties. The new belt buckle was introduced in January 1936 to replace the old *Reichswehr* pattern. It showed the *Wehrmachts-Adler* - the Army pattern

folded-wing eagle and swastika - surrounded by an oakleaf spray and the legend *Gott Mit Uns* ("God With Us") on a pebbled-finish plate. The black leather belt was 4.5cm wide, with a hook at one end and a leather tongue at the other; the buckle had two rear prongs which engaged a double line of size adjustment holes in the tongue.

The ammunition pouches for the service rifle were made as a triple set, each compartment holding two five-round clips, a total of 30 rounds per pouch set; each soldier was issued two pouch sets (except for some second line troops, who received only one). The triple pouch set was attached by two belt loops at the rear, and there was a D-ring at the top rear for attachment to the hooks on the supporting braces. The Mauser S84/98 bayonet is also carried on the belt, the wooden grips indicating early manufacture. The bayonet frog is the early pattern in black leather; later patterns were required to have a retaining strap around the grip.

With the memory of World War I still vivid, every soldier was issued with a gasmask. The M38 *Gasmaske* was carried in a cylindrical, fluted metal canister which was slung across the body on a canvas strap and retained by a short hook-strap clipped to the rear of the belt order (see pages 120-121).

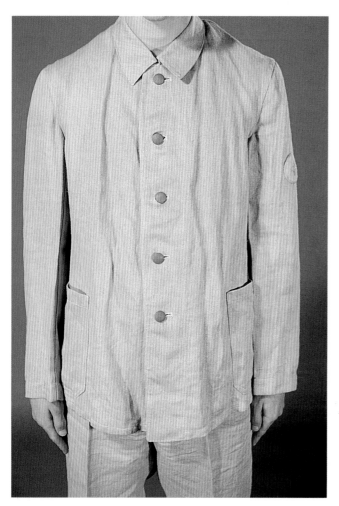

Left
The loose, simple shape of the Drillichanzug jacket echoes its ancestry in the basically similar fatigue garments of unbleached canvas worn by Continental armies since at least the beginning of the 19th century. The single adornment is the rank patch sewn to the upper left sleeve, in this case the star of an Oberschütze or Senior Private. While this jacket is in mint condition, various shades are encountered due to frequent washing.

Bottom
Interior of the drill jacket; there is no lining to this jacket or to the matching trousers. Note the split rings which secure the buttons, and the drawstring at the rear of the jacket to adjust fit.

Immediately below
The jacket is marked Kleiderfabrik ("clothing fabric") Seeifhennersdorf E40 ("Erfurt 1940"). The trousers carry the stamp of M.A.Petersen, the location being illegible.

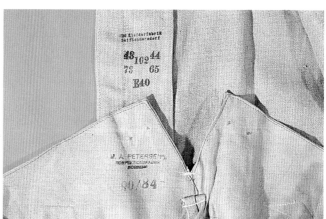

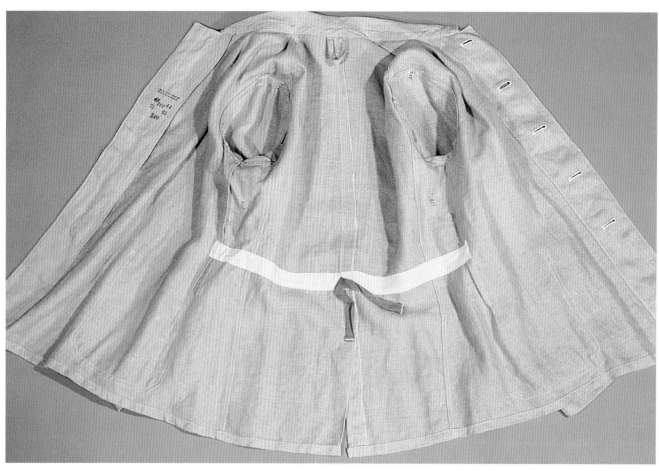

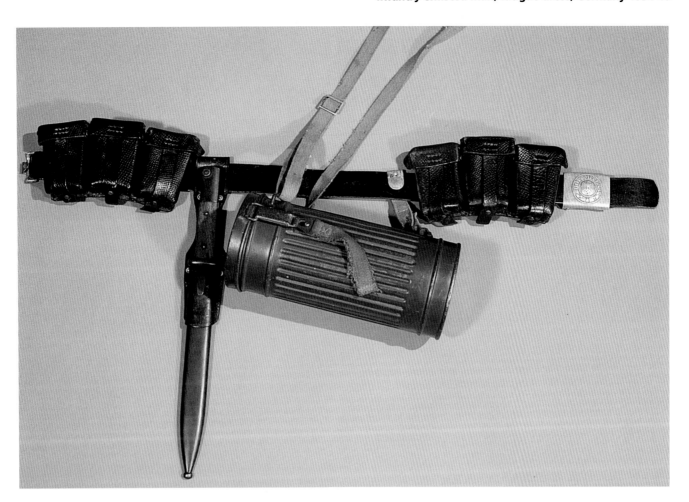

Top
Light belt order: the standard enlisted man's belt with M36 buckle, two triple sets of Model 1911 rifle ammunition pouches in pebbled-finish black leather, the S84/98 bayonet in its black leather frog; and the M38 gasmask in its canister.

Above left
The Army belt buckle introduced in January 1936 was to remain the standard issue for all enlisted men throughout the war. Materials used vary between steel and aluminium, with several manufacturer's variations.

Above right
"Dice-shakers" - the standard Army marching boots which were worn throughout the war by those who could get them, though replaced as official issue from 1940 onwards by laced ankle boots, in order to save on leather.

(5) Artillery officer, greatcoat service dress, Poland 1939

The greatcoat was introduced in 1933 and was the main cold weather garment. It was of the same basic pattern for officers and enlisted ranks, the only differences being in the quality of the fabric and a few minor details of construction. The rank and branch of service of the wearer were denoted by the addition of shoulder straps as worn on the tunic. The deep 9cm falling collar was in the same cloth as the body of the coat during the *Reichsheer* period, its colour being changed to dark green from September 1935.

The greatcoat was worn, when required by the weather, for all duties from training to parades. The pre-war greatcoat was superior to its successors in the quality of the fabric and, to a lesser extent, the workmanship. During the war years economies were introduced, and the superior woollen cloth initially used was steadily degraded with substitute materials. At the earliest stage of the war, before the German Army encountered the very extreme winter conditions of the Eastern Front, the greatcoat was shown to be a completely adequate item of winter clothing.

The greatcoat (*Mantel*) was a double-breasted garment cut from a grey-green woollen fabric. The front had two rows of six uniform buttons, with a single buttonhole on the inner panel at the waist to secure the inside. There was a slanted slash pocket with a rounded flap on each hip, and the sleeves were finished in a deep French cuff (23cm for officers). Across the rear of the waist was an adjustable half-belt with two buttons and buttonholes. The greatcoat had a central rear pleat running from the collar to the hem of the skirt; on dress coats this was sewn closed from collar to half-belt, but on the service grade greatcoat it was left open. From the waist downwards the pleat incorporated a skirt vent which could be closed with four horn buttons, or left open for greater freedom of movement. The collar was secured by a single hook and eye. Underneath the left side of the collar a cloth tab was fixed by two buttons; this could be fastened across to a button under the right collar, supporting the turned-up collar around the chin in bad weather.

The lining of this coat is made from a grey ribbed cotton and covers the inside from the waist upwards, as well as the sleeves; this incorporates a pocket inside the left breast. At each hip there is a vertical vent to allow the belt support hooks of the tunic to pass through. This issue coat has had a suspender strap for the dagger or sword retrospectively added, together with the pocket vent for the hanger to pass through. The maker's mark is for a manufacturer (illegible) in Stettin and is dated 1939. The shoulder straps for the rank of *Leutnant* are of the sewn-in type typical of this early date; they display the red *Waffenfarbe* of the Artillery, and the regimental number "284" stamped in gilt-coloured metal.

This officer's *Schirmmütze* has a crown in ribbed field-grey tricot (*Trikotstoff*), which was the regulation issue material. Both the crown seam and the dark green band bear red wool *Waffenfarbe* piping. The eagle and oakwreath badges are both stamped from light silver-coloured alloy; while early badges were stamped from German silver, this was stopped in late 1935. Double woven aluminium thread cords are secured by two small pebbled-finish buttons; the peak is of vulcanised fibre lacquered to a high gloss. The lining is of grey ribbed silk-effect material with a beige leather

sweatband. The celluloid sweatshield is marked "Original Schellenburg Stirndruckfrei Sonderklasse" and carries the maker's trademark. The term "Stirndruckfrei" refers to a system of reducing pressure on the forehead by a rubber strip glued to the inside of the sweatband at the front.

The *Leutnant* is wearing the M34 officer's service belt. The belt was generally 5cm wide, in a light brown colour, although some variation in width and colour was allowed. The rectangular, open-faced buckle of white metal had two prongs, and a lightly pebbled finish. A cross strap was originally worn with the belt, passing diagonally over the right shoulder to support the weight of a sidearm on the left hip; however, this strap was officially abandoned from September 1939. The *Leutnant* wears a holster for the Luger P08 semi-automatic, which was the official service pistol until production was stopped in 1943 in favour of the Walther P38. One of many slightly differing variants of the M35 report/map case is also worn on the belt; and buttoned to the front of his coat is one of the most common field torches. He is examining a Polish Army service cap.

Right
The grey ribbed tricot material used in this Schirmmütze will be encountered in issue service caps of enlisted and junior officer grades. Note that this example has both badges in the regulation issue stamped white metal alloy.

Below right
Grey silk-effect material is used to line the inside top of the crown, with an unusual change to field-green material around the sides. Note the manufacturer's details on the sweatshield; and the ventilation perforations in the sweatband.

Left
This is the first pattern of greatcoat worn by the German Army during the war years, most immediately distinguished by the dark green collar. Note that the quality of both materials and workmanship is high.

Opposite top
The coat is lined from the waist upwards. Note the hanging pockets below the waist; the pocket in the lining of the left breast; the hemmed vents each side in the rear of the waist for the tunic's belt support hooks; the dagger hanger strap and pocket aperture; and the small buttons to fasten the central rear skirt vent.

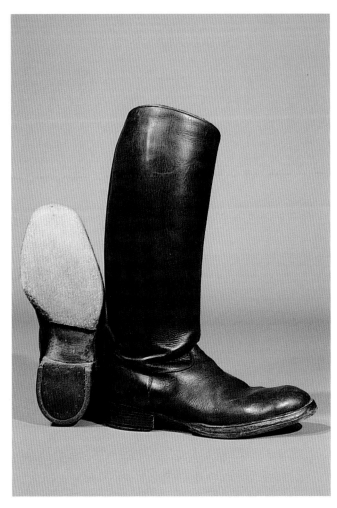

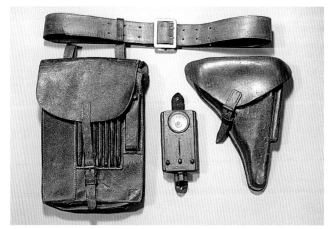

Left
The officer's riding boot (Reitstiefel) had a longer, straighter shaft than the marching boot, and this was usually stiffened from the ankle upwards. Some boots, like these, had metal heel plates.

Above
The M34 officer's service belt; the holster for the Luger P08 pistol; and one of many slight manufacturers' variations on the basic pattern of M35 map case, here in pebbled-finish black leather and stamped "nka 39" - a dated maker's Herstellungszeichen or identifying code. The battery-operated Daimon torch has a buttonhole tab for handy attachment to the uniform; three slides cover the bulb with red, green or blue filters for signalling.

(6) Infantry NCO, combat dress, France 1940

The Infantry were called *König aller Waffen* ("the king of all arms"). Having stormed into the Low Countries on 10 May 1940, the German armed forces crossed the French border further south on the Meuse on the 12th. Against locally determined but generally confused opposition, 119 German divisions cut rapidly through the defenders' lines, with Rommel's 7th Panzer Division finishing the first day 13 kilometres south of the Somme river; by 25 May the leading tank units were on the Channel coast at Boulogne. Whilst much was made in the press of the spectacular advances of the Armoured Divisions, few realised that the hardest fighting was done by the accompanying footsoldiers.

The German infantryman went to war in France with basically the same uniform and equipment used in the Polish campaign of the previous year; and despite many improvements and alterations of detail, the outline appearance of the German *Landser* had many echoes of his predecessors who had last fought in France in 1918.

The M35 field blouse was a modification of the April 1933 pattern, with the addition from September 1935 of the dark green collar facing. It had four patch pockets with box pleats, covered by scalloped flaps secured by single buttons. The front was closed by five pebbled-finish buttons and a single hook and eye (*Umlegekragen*) at the dark green fall collar. The cuffs had a rear vent (*Ärmelschlitz*) at the base with two concealed adjustment buttons. The lining in pre- and early war tunics was of a grey cotton drill material; the front and back panels were lined from 1936 onward. There were usually four sets of holes around the waist of the tunic, through which were passed the belt support hooks (*Seitenhaken*) which were mounted in hanging tabs attached to the lining, the theory being the distribution of weight evenly around the waist.

This particular tunic only has two of these tabs at the back, due to re-tailoring to reduce the size of the chest to allow re-issue at a later date. The tunic carries two sets of markings: the original sizes and "B39" (for the Berlin *Heeresbekleidungsamt* or Army Clothing Office, 1939) have been obscured and replaced with a size marking with a smaller chest measurement. The corresponding markings below show the original manufacturer "Herfa Berlin 034 Gubener Str.47", with the later post-1942 state manufacturing code number (*Reichsbetriebnummer*) above this. A pocket for wound dressings is sewn inside the front right skirt panel; and there are three resin (sometimes cardboard) buttons at the collar for attaching a neckband liner (*Kragenbinde*).

The collar patches are the 1938 standard *Einheitslitzen* applied directly to the collar without backing patches; the breast eagle is the early pattern machine-woven in white cotton on dark green badge cloth. The shoulder straps display the rank of *Stabsfeldwebel* (Staff Sergeant Major) with the NCO's 9mm *Tresse* braid and three silver stars, on the early dark green base. The strap is retained by a tongue on the underside which passes through a cloth loop ("bridle") on the tunic shoulder, tongue and strap both engaging the uniform button close to the neck. The silver *Tresse* was also applied around the bottom and front edges of the collar for

NCO ranks. This uniform, belonging to a soldier from Berlin, retains his original awards: the Iron Cross 1st Class, the Infantry Assault Badge (and, deliberately obscured in these photographs, the Kuban Shield on the sleeve, awarded in September 1943 for the fierce fighting in the Kuban bridgehead on the Russian Front).

The service trousers were manufactured in stone-grey (*Steingrau*) until 1940; thereafter they were cut from the basic field-grey cloth. The waist was cut higher at the back than the front, and there was a horizontal adjustment tab at the rear. The fly front usually closed with five buttons, and suspender (braces) attachment buttons were provided inside the waistband. There were two slash pockets at the hips and one at the right rear, each closed by a single button; a small patch fob pocket was provided at the right groin with a watch chain retaining tab above. The leg was cut straight.

The M35 steel helmet still retains the national tricolour shield transfer on the right side, although this was ordered removed during 1940. The basic fighting belt order is worn, with M31 breadbag (haversack), field flask with cup, and messtins. At the beginning of the war there was a shortage of sub-machine guns, and NCOs usually carried the rifle at this early date; he also carries here an M24 "stick" hand grenade.

Above left
The M35 helmet, retaining the national tricolour shield at this early date, but with wartime "rough" paint finish. Helmets were supplied from the factories painted inside and out in a variety of differing field- and slate-grey finishes. In the field the surface was often further roughened and camouflaged with smeared-on mud.

Above
The M35 tunic, the first pattern used during the war years, distinguished by the pre-war dark green collar. The generally superior finish is quite apparent in this photograph. Note the gentle scallop of the pocket flaps.

Left
The insignia. The 9mm Tresse braiding around the collar and shoulder straps denoted all NCOs from the rank of Unteroffizier upwards; the continuation of the braid across the butt of the straps, all NCOs from Unterfeldwebel upwards; and these three silver stars, the rank of Stabsfeldwebel. The white Infantry Waffenfarbe appears only as outer shoulder strap piping.

Above
The tunic lining, while in the standard material, has been changed due to the tailoring alterations carried out during the war. The two front belt hook tabs have been removed, and new pocket stitching is also discernible. Note the field dressing pocket on the lower right panel; and the buttoned-in neckband liner.

Below left
The interesting markings in this tunic: the upper size stampings have been obscured and re-stamped after alteration. At the bottom is the original maker's stamp, which is surmounted by the re-issue Reichsbetriebnummer, dating the alterations as post-1942.

Below
The M34 knapsack pack (Tornister 34) had integral shoulder straps, unlike its M39 replacement which attached directly to the combat braces. Blanket, greatcoat, and camouflage-printed Zeltbahn 31 shelter section/poncho could be rolled and strapped to three pairs of leather loops on the top and side surfaces. The body was made of canvas in various shades of brown or green; the outer flap was normally covered with unshaven calf- or horse-hide, though pre-war plain canvas flaps are known. The knapsack was issued to all dismounted troops, but was not generally worn in combat, being left with the unit baggage transport.

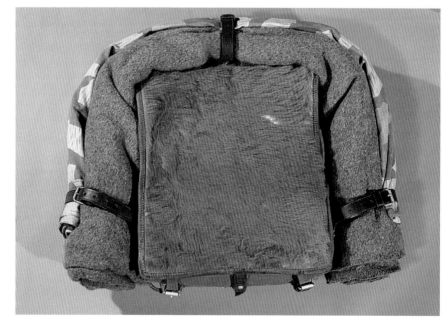

(7) Administrative Official, service dress, France 1940-41

The position of "armed forces official" (*Wehrmachtbeamte*) was created to free line officers from time-consuming administrative duties, and to harness the necessary special skills of personnel who might not be suitable for line service. Officials wore Army uniform and were subject to military discipline, but did not have the same status as serving soldiers. They bore ranks equivalent to service grades from NCO up to general officer, being appointed to these according to their educational level and qualifications. Their rank table comprised four career grade classifications: high, elevated, medium, and lower grade. High grade and elevated career officials held officer rank; medium covered NCOs with the possibility of attaining officer rank within this grade; and lower career covered NCO ranks. The service provided officials qualified in a wide variety of specialist fields, e.g.judiciary, food supply, teaching, foreign languages, chemistry, psychology, hospital administration, veterinary medecine, dentistry, survey and mapping, etc. Without the expertise of these usually unsung professionals the daily management of the Army would have been impossible.

Administrative officials were responsible for the procurement of their own uniform, and were provided with an allowance for this purpose. They could also purchase issue items from Army depots, but in the early war period uniforms were usually tailor-made. The example illustrated here is of the finest quality, cut from a fine blended wool and following the service tunic design. It has four patch pockets with box pleats, covered by stylishly scalloped flaps. Instead of the usual five front buttons this tunic has six, and all buttons are in bright silver finish. The sleeves are finished with deep turned-back French cuffs; the stiffened collar is in dark green badge cloth, cut to a fashionable long point, and is secured with two hooks. The full lining is cut from a silver-grey satin, with an internal pocket in the left breast; the sleeves are fully lined with a white pin-striped cotton; and the shoulders have been padded to improve the appearance.

The insignia are also of the highest quality hand-embroidered bullion; the national eagle on the breast even has the swastika worked in gold wire thread - a strictly non-regulation touch. The shoulder straps and collar patches indicate an official of elevated career. The shoulder straps carry the rank equivalent of *Oberleutnant*, and the "HV" cipher (*Heeresverwaltungs*, "Army administration") worn by all officials since December 1934. The *Waffenfarbe* for officials was dark green with a secondary colour (*Nebenfarbe*) indicating the particular area of specialisation; in this case the secondary underlay is white, indicating one of a number of paymaster, garrisoning or victualling duties. The collar patches are in the style for all officials of elevated career, with the outer piping in the secondary colour. This official has been awarded the War Merit Cross (*Kreigsverdienstkreuz*) in Silver with Swords; the KVK was the non-combatant's equivalent of the Iron Cross series of awards.

The M38 field cap for officers was introduced in December 1938 to replace the "old style" field cap. It was simply an officer's version of the M34 field cap for enlisted ranks, with the same oval profile, but with a higher crown and a more pronounced scallop at the front of the fold-down flap which ran around the body; there was a ventilation eyelet above the flap at either side. The officer's *Feldmütze* was usually of a

finer grade material, but this example is one purchased from the Army and is not representative of private purchase quality. The top edges of the crown and the front scallop are piped in silver-coloured bullion, denoting officer rank (that of general officers being in gold bullion). The eagle badge is machine-woven in silver thread on a dark green backing; the tricolour national cockade (*Reichskokade*) is embroidered as a raised boss in bullion, surrounded by a soutache (inverted chevron) of "Russia braid" in the dark green primary *Waffenfarbe* (the use of the soutache was abolished in July 1942). The grey cotton drill lining has a faint size marking, and the trademark "Mützenfabrik" stamped in the top.

At this period the officer's riding breeches are still in stone-grey; they are privately tailored, to high quality, with a fashionably pronounced flare at the thigh. They have one slash pocket at each hip and one at the right rear with a flap, each secured by a button; there is also a small slash fob pocket at the right groin. Buttons and tabs are provided for the use of braces, and all buttons are of brown bakelite. The fly is secured by four buttons, with a horizontal hook at the waistband. The legs are closed with a length of lacing and a calf flap with four buttons.

Above left
The M38 Feldmütze - the "new style field cap for officers" - followed the pattern set by the M34 enlisted ranks' cap. This example is of issue quality. Note the silver cord piping identifying commissioned rank, the tricolour cockade worked as a raised boss in bullion thread and felt, and the silver thread officer's eagle and swastika badge.

Above
The cap lining, of average quality in grey twill; note the stitched reinforcement around the ventilation eyelets. Some privately purchased examples will be found in superior "moleskin" material, with high quality lining and a partial sweatband of thin leather in the forehead area.

Left
This official's tunic displays the high quality tailoring of the best private purchase uniforms. The material is a soft wool blend; the very pointed collar and deeply turned back French cuffs are other features of fashionable tailoring.

Top
The superb hand-embroidered bullion thread insignia of an official of elevated career. Note the gold thread swastika of the breast eagle - an individual affectation; and the sewn-in shoulder straps with the Army official's gilt "HV" cipher, a single rank star, and white-over-dark green double underlay.

Above
The tunic is lined with a quality silver-grey satin material. Despite being privately tailored it lacks some often-seen features such as a waist adjustment belt and dagger hanger vent.

Right
The stone-grey breeches, showing the fittings for braces, the slanted pockets, and the lace and button closure at the calf.

(8) Armoured Troops enlisted man, vehicle service dress, France 1940

The "special" black *Panzer* uniform (*Sonderbekleidung*) introduced for tank troops in 1934 was a dramatic departure from contemporary German Army uniform design. Practical consideration given to the requirements of the wearer's duties led to a unique style of uniform. The jacket was short and close-fitting, without external pockets, so as to prevent snagging on the many protrusions inside an armoured vehicle; it was deeply double-breasted, allowing for the breast to be buttoned across for extra warmth; and was black in colour, to hide oil stains. Apart from the protective *Panzer* beret (*Schutzmütze*), which was abandoned as early as 1941, headdress followed standard Army patterns throughout the war, but field caps were produced in black cloth. The uniform was intended to be worn only when working with the armoured vehicle; however, because of its dashing appearance this restriction was soon ignored, and at the end of 1940 it became the everyday service uniform of the *Panzerwaffe*.

The jacket shown here was privately tailored in Paris, and deviates from the issue jacket in several ways. The first pattern jacket (M34) had a less pointed collar than the second (M36), and did not have the buttons and hook to allow the lapels to be fastened across. The example illustrated has the later pointed collar but has no buttonholes in the lapel. The front closure is, conventionally, secured at the right waist by four plastic or horn buttons behind a slanted fly. The inner, right hand panel of the issue jacket had two buttons which engaged with two tabs on the lining of the left hand panel; this jacket lacks them, though it does have the regular adjustable vent at the base of the sleeve. As is common with tailored jackets, the skirt is several inches shorter than the regulation pattern and the waist has been nipped in to a tight fit. The collar is piped in the rose-pink *Waffenfarbe* of the *Panzertruppe*, as was regulation until late 1942.

The lining of the regulation jacket was grey cotton twill and covered the front panels only. There was a belt hook suspender tab under each armpit, with four slots in the waist for the hook to pass through. There were a horizontal patch pocket inside the right breast and a vertical slash pocket in the left, and an interior waist adjustment tape (see section 26 for photographs of these features). This privately purchased jacket has a tailored full lining in black ribbed satin. The tailor's label reads "Thorn 1. rue de la pépiniére Paris (VIIe)".

The collar patches, peculiar to the Armoured Troops and worn by all ranks on this uniform, are black, lozenge-shaped, and piped in the same rose-pink artificial silk as the collar. The stamped white metal death's-heads are attached by two pins and have been further secured with black thread sewn through the eye and nose sockets. The white-on-black breast eagle is a good early example; after 1939 grey on black was the norm. The black shoulder straps, plain apart from *Waffenfarbe* piping, are of the early sewn-in type. On the upper left sleeve is the single chevron denoting the rank of *Gefreiter* (roughly, Lance-Corporal) in silver *Tresse* on black. The ribbon for the Iron Cross 2nd Class is worn on the lapel, sewn where the buttonhole would normally be set.

The *Schutzmütze* was the only black headgear issued before the outbreak of war. It was a rational design for its time (which pre-dated the provision of radio communication to all

the crew stations of German tanks); but in use it proved unpopular due to its unflattering appearance, and the difficulty of wearing it with radio headphones. The inner body was a large protective skullcap made from rubber with a black wool covering; set around the crown were six rubber ventilation eyelets, and the interior was lined in black oilcloth with a leather sweatband. Inside the crown of the illustrated example is a manufacturer's label for "Carl Halfar Berlin N20 Prinzenallee 74". Over the outside, pulled down to engage with the groove formed by the edge of its prominent padded rim, was worn a black spun wool beret, bearing at the front the national eagle and wreath machine-woven in white thread on black (initially only the wreath was worn, the eagle being added in October 1935).

The vehicle service trousers were produced in the same black wool as the jacket. They had three (occasionally four) slash pockets with scalloped single-button flaps, buttoning forward on the hip pockets, and a small fob pocket at the right groin. The fly had four buttons on the right flap and two at the waist on the left flap; the waistband had an integral cloth belt protruding at the front and secured with a three-prong buckle. The legs were cut generously wide, tapering in at the ankle where a vent was secured by a button and tie-tapes.

Above
The "Panzer beret" consists of a rubber crash cap covered with a spun wool beret. Unpopular for its clumsy appearance, it also made the wearing of radio headphones, with their large rubber pads, extremely inconvenient. With the later extension of radio to all crew stations of German tanks there was a good excuse to discard it in favour of soft fieldcaps; several photos of the 1940 French campaign show the black uniform being worn with the field-grey Feldmütze.

Above
The lining is quite shallow and is covered with black oilcloth. As well as the maker's label this example is marked with the date 1941 stamped on the sweatband. Note the rubber ventilation eyelets just behind the sweatband.

Left
This privately tailored example of the Panzerjacke is approximately six inches shorter than the issue pattern - a popular fashion. The striking appearance which made this uniform so popular among the troops as everyday and walking-out dress is quite apparent.

Opposite top left
Details of the insignia. The death's-head collar patches, recalling the mirliton and shako badges worn by famous 18th and 19th century Prussian Hussar regiments, were unique in the Army at the time of their introduction. The breast eagle is of early quality. Note that all piping is made from rose-pink artificial silk.

Opposite top right
The black vehicle service trousers were of a generous cut to allow free movement in the cramped confines of a tank. Note the pocket flaps, the internal waist belt, and the button and tape fastening of the ankle vent.

Opposite below
While the superior lining of this privately purchased Paris-made jacket is not of the issue type, it is fairly typical of a tailored garment. Note that the positions of the pockets are the same as in the regulation jacket, however.

(9) Infantry officer, NCO Preparatory School staff, Germany 1940-42

Upon the outbreak of war with the Western powers it became apparent to the High Command that an extensive programme of training would be required to build a base non-commissioned officer corps which would allow regular promotion of trained junior leaders into the officer ranks. With this in mind the NCO Preparatory Schools (*Unteroffiziervorschulen*) were created in April 1940. Students were aged from 14 to 17 and were officially classed as civilians, not soldiers, while attending the school. They were given three years of civil education, combined with military education, in order to prepare them for service in the Army. Students wore the basic service uniform but with French cuffs instead of the standard open cuff; distinctions consisted of special collar patches, smooth buttons, and the school's cipher on the shoulder straps - a Gothic "UV" and a Roman numeral denoting the school area. They also wore the *"Unteroffiziervorschule"* cuff-title on the lower right sleeve. Staff of the schools wore the uniform of their previous posting, with the addition of the shoulder cipher and cuff-title.

This *Oberstleutnant* (Lieutenant-Colonel) wears an old style service tunic. This *Reichswehr* pattern, which was supposed to be used only until March 1942, was popular with senior officers as a mark of long Army service. This tailor-made tunic has two upper patch pockets with pleats and scalloped flaps; the lower pair are the slash type and are cut at a slant, also with scalloped flaps. The pointed collar is closed by two hooks and was originally faced with field-grey cloth, but this was ordered changed to dark green in September 1935. The front of the tunic closes with eight buttons, and both the inner and outer panels are piped down the front edge in the wearer's *Waffenfarbe*. The rear of the tunic is cut in the traditional manner, with rear seams arching down from the shoulders to the small of the back where two belt supporting buttons are mounted. Inside the rear skirt are two concealed pockets in the same fashion as the dress tunic. The sleeves are finished with the usual French cuffs; the body is cut to fit closely at the waist. The lining is typical of private tailoring, with a ribbed satin material, the inclusion of a waist belt and the provision of a slot at the lower left pocket for the hanger of a dagger or sword.

The insignia are of high quality bright silver hand embroidery. The collar patches are the standard officer's pattern *Litzen*, the bars with Infantry white *Waffenfarbe* "lights"; the breast eagle is a very fine hand-embroidered example. The plaited silver cord shoulder straps of field rank bear the single gilt star of an *Oberstleutnant* ; as a rule, they were always of the sewn-in type on these tunics. The "UV" cipher for the *Unteroffiziervorschule* is also displayed; while it was correct for officers to wear these in gilt, it was not uncommon for the NCO's German silver type to be worn (as here) if more readily available. The cuff-title bore the legend *"Unteroffiziervorschule"* machine-woven in silver Gothic script on a dark field-green backing with a silver border. The awards worn here consist of the ribbon for the Iron Cross 2nd class, the pin-back Iron Cross 1st Class, and the Wound Badge in black. A ribbon bar above the pocket displays World War I and II awards. The belt seen here is also an early private purchase type, wider than later patterns.

The field cap was introduced in March 1934 and was designated the "old style officer's field cap" (*Offizierfeldmütze älterer Art*) in 1938, when it was officially superseded by the boat-shaped field cap. This old pattern remained extremely popular with all officer ranks, however, and was seen in use well past the official wear-out date of April 1942. The field-grey crown and dark green band were only slightly stiffened, with no spine or metal stiffener, and the peak was made of semi-soft leather. This allowed the cap to be folded for carrying, and also gave it the popular crushed, "front line" look. The interior usually had no celluloid sweatshield, any maker's names being printed directly on the lining; the sweatband was made of either thin leather or a cardboard leatherette. The eagle and wreath insignia were flat, machine-woven in silver thread on a dark green backing, which was either machine- or hand-sewn in place. There were no chin cords or side buttons, although many officers added these later in order to continue wearing the cap after the wear-out date.

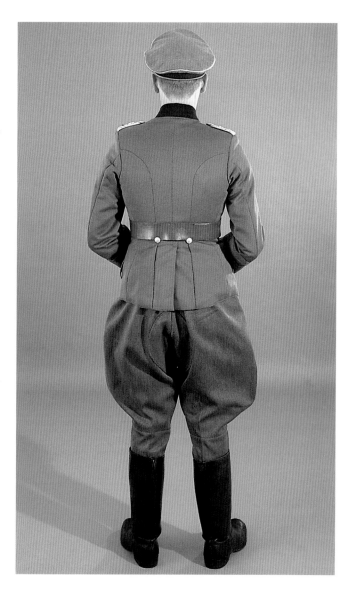

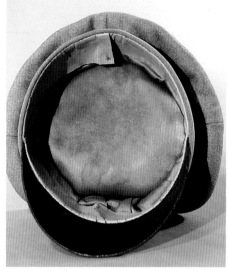

Above left
The "old style officer's field cap"; the soft crown and non-rigid black leather peak are evident here. Note the flat woven insignia, and the lack of chin cords on this pattern of cap.

Above
The lining of this cap is in silver-grey satin-effect material and has no manufacturer's trademark. The sweatband has discoloured from a buff to a grey colour, and is made from a composite leatherette.

Left
The "old style" service tunic differs outwardly from its successors in having slanted slash skirt pockets, piping down the front edges, and eight front buttons. Note the tailored fit at the waist

Left
This is a typical lining for a tailored tunic. There are concealed internal pockets either side of the rear skirt vent. Note the waist adjustment belt and the dagger hanger slit.

Left
The "Unteroffiziervorschule" cuff-title was worn by all students and staff on the right cuff of the service tunic and greatcoat.

Left
The fine quality of these early insignia is apparent. Note the non-regulation but not uncommon use of a German silver NCO's pattern shoulder strap cipher in place of the gilt officer's pattern.

(10) Infantry officer, service dress, France 1940-41

hile most enlisted men were issued with their uniforms and field equipment on joining the Army, officers, officials and various specialists were required to purchase these items themselves. To assist in this they were granted a clothing allowance on joining and thereafter received additional amounts for upkeep on a monthly basis. Clothing was purchased either from the "officers' clothing fund" (*Offizier Kleiderkasse*), or from one of the large number of private tailors and military outfitters. Purchases were made with uniform vouchers (*Uniformbezugschein*) issued by the Army. All privately purchased items had to closely reflect the design and colour of the issue items in order to maintain uniformity.

The quality of privately tailored uniforms, particularly before the war, was generally high. With the growing duration of commitment to combat many officers either began to have more "utility" field dress made, or resorted to purchasing issue tunics, with appropriate insignia fitted, for field use (see sections 12 and 23). For the first year of war with Russia quality remained generally high; from about mid-1942, due to the practical effects of lengthy front line service, growing economic pressures and increasing shortages of materials, the general appearance of the officer corps began to show a marked decline.

The uniform illustrated is a fine example of pre- to early war tailored tunics. It is manufactured from a high quality blended wool, smooth in appearance and soft to the touch. The colour is the greyer shade which was seen mostly before the war, later being superseded by greener tones of field-grey. The four box-pleated patch pockets with scalloped flaps are sewn so as to remain flush to the body of the tunic; all seams are of a distinctly "ridged" profile. The front closure has six buttons, regarded as more fashionable than the regular five; nevertheless, these are painted green for a "field" look. The French cuffs are much deeper than normal, and the waist is closely fitted above the hips. The internally stiffened collar, faced in dark green badge cloth, is cut to sit high; it has pronounced points, and two fastening hooks instead of one. On the inside of the collar are three butterfly hooks for the fitting of a collar liner (*Kragenbinde*); buttons, or shirt-type studs, may also be found in this position. The lining, of a dark grey ribbed satin-effect material, covers the entire inside surface; there is an internal left breast pocket, and a vent for the dagger or sword hanger inside the lower left pocket. The sleeves are lined with the pin-striped cotton characteristic of quality private tailoring.

The insignia are of the early quality which is to be expected. The shoulder straps for *Leutnant* (Second Lieutenant) are of the pre-war sewn-in type with fine white wool *Waffenfarbe* underlay; it is not easy to discern in these photographs, but the metallic cord is in fact of the more matt, oxydized silver finish characteristic of wartime examples. The collar *Litzen* are hand-embroidered over a cardboard pattern, also with white Infantry *Waffenfarbe*. The breast eagle, whilst standard, is a fine quality hand-embroidered example. The awards worn on this tunic are pinned through loops sewn to the left breast pocket. They are the Iron Cross 1st Class, the Infantry Assault Badge, and the Wound Badge in black.

The *Schirmmütze* is an early quality example from the firm of

Peter Küpper, which traded under the name "Peküro". It has a fine grade "Eskimo" (blended wool) top in early light grey, stiffened with a wire which runs through the white crown seam piping and retains the *Sattelform* (saddle shape). The peak is made not from the usual *Vulkanfibre* but from a very strong treated card. This cap has a caramel-coloured lining made of waterproof cotton, and carries the Peküro trademark on the sweatshield, as well as "Stirndruckfrei Deutsches Reichspatent", referring to the patented system for reducing pressure on the forehead. The silver-coloured bullion chin cords are attached by two small silver pebbled-finish buttons. The national eagle is stamped from light metal, although embroidered versions were also commonly used. The wreath and cockade came in three patterns: all metal; all embroidered; or, as usually encountered on the more expensive private purchase caps, this combination of embroidered wreath with metal cockade.

This officer wears ribbed twill breeches in stone-grey; an early light brown service belt; and a small frame pistol holster - various light semi-automatics, notably the Walther PPK, were often preferred to the heavier 9mm service weapons.

Above left
This service cap is representative of early quality and finish. The crown is in a light grey and is stiffened to conform to the "saddle" shape. Note the embroidered wreath with a metal cockade applied.

Above
The cap lining is of a waterproofed cotton with the standard transparent sweatshield, stamped here with the "Peküro" trademark. Note the small strip of black velvet added for comfort around the outer edge of the sweatband, a feature of some expensive caps.

Left
The quality features of good tailoring are seen here. Note the pointed collar, the flat sit of the pockets, the deep cuffs and the high quality insignia.

Right
The sewn-in shoulder straps, commonly found on pre-war and privately tailored wartime tunics, though usually with brighter silver cord. The collar patches and breast eagle are hand-embroidered, the former over card patterns.

Opposite top
The tunic lining is made from dark grey satin, with the usual feature of a dagger hanger access slot through to the lower left pocket. Note the collar liner attachments.

Above
The thread loops for the pins of the awards cluster them very closely together. Note that they were always worn in order of grade, with the highest award at the top - here, the Iron Cross 1st Class (for conspicuous bravery or leadership in combat), above the Infantry Assault Badge (basically awarded to officers and men who had taken part in at least three different infantry attacks), and the black Wound Badge (marking one and two wounds suffered in combat).

(11) Cavalry enlisted man, combat dress, Russia 1941-43

Despite the common impression of a highly mechanised army, mounted units were an integral part of the *Heer* throughout World War II. A huge proportion of the Army's supplies were carried not by motorised transport but by columns of horse-drawn wagons, which were an integrated part of almost every unit's structure. During the 1930s the Army reduced its mounted cavalry units from three divisions to a single brigade, such troops generally being converted to the mechanised reconnaissance role. During the war, however, the mounted cavalry strength grew once more to several divisions, and mounted troops were found in signals, reconnaissance, artillery, supply, and even in infantry units where they acted as despatch riders. On the Eastern Front the huge expanses of almost roadless terrain, and the nature of some operations - notably anti-partisan security duties behind the front lines - offered mounted cavalry a genuinely useful role.

The uniform for mounted troops was the same as for the rest of the Army with the addition of a couple of items: as well as the standard issue trousers mounted troops received riding breeches, and riding boots instead of marching boots.

The M40 field blouse was introduced in May 1940 as the first of a series of economy measures which would alter the appearance of the German soldier as the war progressed. The collar, and the body of the shoulder straps, were now to be in the same field-grey cloth as the rest of the uniform rather than in dark green badge cloth. The tunic remained otherwise unchanged, with four pleated patch pockets and a five-button closure, and adjustable vents at the base of the cuff; the scallop of the pocket flaps was retained, with a more pronounced curve being a feature of early tunics. While the order for this pattern tunic was officially announced in May 1940, it is interesting to note that this illustrated example was manufactured in Hannover in 1939, and that photographic evidence also suggests some 1939 manufacture. At this early stage of the war the *Feldbluse* displays a full lining of grey cotton drill.

The collar patches seen here were introduced in November 1938, and were used by all branches of service on the field blouse. The breast eagle is the pattern seen at the start of the war, worked in white cotton instead of the later grey colour. While field-grey shoulder straps had been introduced by this time the early dark green pattern were still seen in use right up until the end of the war.

The field service trousers remained unchanged, but as a member of a mounted unit this man has been issued the riding breeches. These remained basically the same throughout the war, the only change being the substitution, in some cases, of a cloth doubling for natural brown or slate-grey leather in the seat reinforcement, which covered the generously cut seat area and extended down the inside legs. The breeches had three slash pockets with buttons and a fob pocket at the right groin; they were high cut at the rear, with a horizontal adjustment tab and buttons for the fitting of braces (suspenders); issue breeches fastened at the ankle with three buttons. All members of mounted units received long-shafted riding boots as a priority throughout the war; these were usually worn with the nickel plated steel M31 spurs (*Anschnallsporen*), with black leather straps.

The basic belt order is worn here, with the Cavalry belt suspenders (*Kavallerie-Tragegurt*); these braces did not feature the D-rings and pack straps of the dismounted pattern, as riders were not required to wear a knapsack - they are commonly referred to as "parade" braces. The bayonet frog for mounted personnel (*Seitengewehrtasche für Berittene*) had a hilt retaining strap; this feature was retrospectively ordered for all troops from January 1939, but was not universally seen even by 1945.

The standard issue saddle during the war was the M25 (*Armeesattel 25*), which was a lightweight, tan leather saddle on a timber frame. The saddle bags are the 1934 pattern (*Packtaschen 34*) which comprised three pieces: a left and a right bag with a separate coupling device. The left bag held the requirements of the horse, the right the rider's personal kit; this rider's bag was fitted with two pack straps, enabling the rider to wear it when dismounted. They were attached to the coupling plate by use of a U-shaped bracket, and the whole assembly was similarly attached to the front of the saddle. There were various strapping points to the rear of the saddle, enabling the bedroll, *Zeltbahn* and other pieces of kit to be strapped on. A grey blanket was used between the saddle and the horse.

Above

The M40 Feldbluse; the reproduction of the cut of the M36 service tunic (Heeres Dienstanzug Modell 1936) can easily be seen, the only difference being the field-grey collar. Note the fairly pronounced shape of these early manufacture pocket flaps; this example was in fact made as early as 1939.

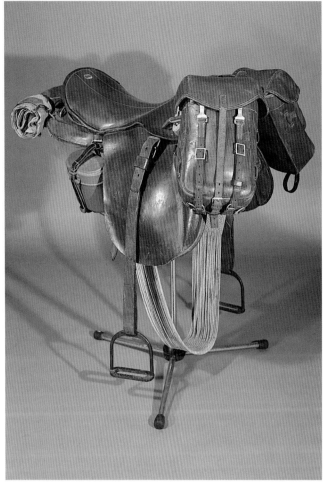

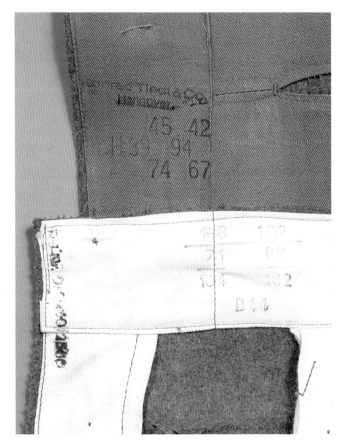

Above
These breeches were issued to all mounted personnel, regardless of rank. Note that during the war the leather seat reinforcement was sometimes replaced by a doubled area of the same cloth as the rest of the garment.

Opposite top right
This is the early pattern of insignia as seen at the beginning of the war; note that the workmanship on all items is superior, the only economic concession being the loss of a backing to the collar patches.
The shoulder straps are piped in the golden-yellow Waffenfarbe of the Cavalry.

Left
The tunic lining in drab grey cotton drill seen here is an indication of early manufacture. Note that the four belt support hooks were hung directly through the body of the tunic at the eyelets rather than being mounted on hanging tabs.

Above right
The Army Model 1925 saddle is seen here with the M34 saddle bags, which were the most commonly used. Note the stowage of the pack straps, for dismounted use, on the front of the rider's (nearside) bag; the rope girth strap; and the positioning of gear at the rear of the saddle.

Right
This tunic, despite being an M40 pattern, is marked to "Konrad Tiedt & Co Hannover H 39", indicating that this modification to the 1936 pattern was already being carried out at this earlier date. The breeches are marked "B44 " (for Berlin 1944) but are identical to earlier patterns.

(12) Cavalry officer, service dress, Russia 1941-44

As the war with Russia unfolded it became clear that the wear and tear on the service dress was going to be greater than in previous campaigns. Officers who had previously worn in the field uniforms which were tailor-made at their own expense began drawing the standard issue enlisted ranks' tunic from their unit stores; they were entitled to do so at no expense, under an order of October 1939 which stated that they were to wear standard issue garments in a combat zone. Some chose to modify the tunic only by adding the officer's service grade insignia; others had the tunics modified by a tailor to give them the appearance of the officer's pattern. Apart from the change-over of insignia there were two alterations which usually accomplished this. The field-grey collar was faced with dark green badge cloth; and - in some instances - the sleeve was altered to replace the adjustable cuff vent (*Ärmelschlitz*) with the officer's turned-back French cuff (*Rollunschlag*).

The tunic illustrated started life as a standard issue 1940 pattern soldier's field blouse manufactured in 1941. After issue from unit stores its owner had cosmetic alterations made to bring it up to officer grade appearance. The field-grey collar facing material has been removed and replaced with the dark green badge cloth used on the pre-war tunic; and the cuff vents have been closed and deep French cuffs added, from material which is an almost but not quite perfect match. (The turned-back cuffs were not purely a mark of status; officers often slipped small documents, etc. into them like extra pockets.) The inside of the tunic shows evidence of extensive work; all the belt support hook tabs have been removed, and the rear panel seams have been pulled in to give the waist a better fit. The skirt has also been shortened in keeping with fashion, and this has meant the removal and re-sewing of the bottom pockets.

The insignia consist of the hand-embroidered officer's collar *Litzen*, with "lights" of golden-yellow Cavalry *Waffenfarbe*, and the embroidered officer's breast eagle. The shoulder straps are of the sewn-in type, the original bridles for attaching slip-on straps being removed. The rank star of *Oberleutnant* and the unit designation are in white metal with a gold-coloured wash; the Gothic letter "L" (for Lehr) identified instructional units. The straps are of the subdued silver thread characteristic of wartime manufacture, on golden-yellow underlay. On the left breast pocket are the Iron Cross 1st Class, the *Allgemeines Sturmabzeichen* (General Assault Badge, awarded for participation in successful attacks by personnel of units other than Infantry and Armour), and the black Wound Badge.

The *Schirmmütze* is constructed from a greener and more "field grade" wool than the examples illustrated earlier, despite being of private purchase *Sonderklasse* quality. The lining is of a fine golden artificial silk, with a ventilated sweatband, and a celluloid sweatshield elaborately marked to the maker Armin Greiner of Bad Warmbrunn and carrying the company trademark with the legend "Spezialhause für Uniformen" ("specialty house for uniforms"). Both badges are of the stamped metal pattern; *Waffenfarbe* crown and band piping and officer's chin cords are conventional.

The riding breeches (*Reiterhose*) illustrated have brown

leather seat reinforcement which has darkened from wear; the same breeches were issued to all ranks (apart from general officers). This pair have a cream linen waistband and pockets. The boots are the officer's type with a moulded leather shaft but a soft ankle for comfort when riding. An order of 1939 stating that officers in the field were to wear the enlisted pattern belt was almost universally ignored. This officer wears the brown field belt, with the full flap M35 report/map case, and a holster for the 9mm Browning Hi-Power pistol which was manufactured for the *Wehrmacht* in occupied Belgium. He is also using the Walther-designed 2.7cm Army flare pistol (*Signalpistole-Heeres Modell*); this was carried in a holster slung from a shoulder strap.

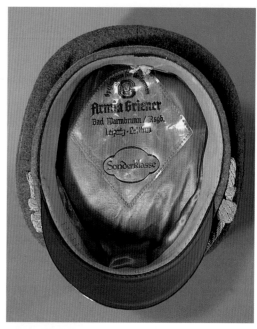

Above left
This "field quality" Cavalry officer's private purchase Schirmmütze, in a greenish shade of field-grey, outwardly follows the pattern set down in regulations.

Above
The cap lining does not comply with the regulations stating that the underside of the peak, the lining material and the sweatband should be in the same colour. Note the elaborately marked manufacturer's sweatshield.

Left
The smarter appearance of this M40 enlisted ranks' field blouse after partial retailoring is evident; but note that the eyelets for the belt support hooks are still present, immediately identifying the tunic's origins "in the ranks".

Opposite top
The gilt-coloured shoulder strap devices - the star of an Oberleutnant (First Lieutenant) and the "L" for Lehr - are pressed in white metal and gilt-washed. Golden-yellow "lights" on the collar lace identify the Cavalry. The thickly worked appearance of the breast eagle is common for hand-embroidered pieces.

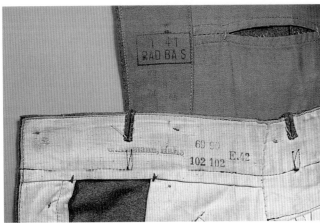

Above
The marking inside the tunic (above) is possibly a unit tailor's stamp with the size numbers faintly present underneath. The breeches (below) are extensively marked, including the manufacturer's, size, and depot stamps (for Erfurt 1942).

Right
This Leuchtpistole- (or Signalpistole-) Heeres Modell, adopted in 1928, was one of two types used throughout the war; the longer-barrelled variant dated from 1935. Note the 2.7cm cartridge, which is notched at the base for identification in the dark. The leather holster has a cup at the base and a strap to hold the cleaning rod, which was quite commonly missing. The narrow shoulder strap engages with two D-rings on the rear.

(13) Artillery enlisted man, winter sentry dress, Russia 1941

When Germany invaded Russia on 22 June 1941, the campaign plan anticipated that before the onset of winter the Red Army could be drawn into battle, encircled and annihilated in western Russia, and Leningrad, Moscow and the Ukraine captured. Despite stunning advances and victories, however, Hitler's meddling over priority objectives left the *Wehrmacht* stalled short of Moscow by the October mud; and in the snows of late November a Russian counter-offensive brought the advance to a halt in the coldest winter in living memory. It was a winter war the Germans were not equipped to handle. During peacetime the issue of winter kit was restricted to the calendar season, and even then the items available were adequate only for winter in temperate climates, not the icy horrors of northern Russia. Casualties from frostbite soon outnumbered those from combat wounds. By their nature, some tasks - particularly static, exposed sentry or outpost duty - were particularly dangerous. The troops improvised in order to survive, by using captured Russian uniforms and boots, by stuffing their uniforms and boots with paper and straw, and by wearing as many layers of clothing as they could find. In Germany there was a hurried public collection of civilian furs and winter clothing by the Winter Relief Organisation (*Winterhilfswerk*) to send to the front.

The watchcoat (*Übermantel*) was introduced from November 1934 to protect vehicle drivers and sentries from the exposure inseparable from these duties. As one of the few suitable items of clothing available, it was used extensively during the first winter in Russia. Based on the service greatcoat, it had additional protective features, and was generously cut and sized to allow it to be worn over the uniform and field equipment (though most soldiers wore the equipment externally). The coat was double-breasted, with front panels of increased width, and had two rows of six buttons. The length was also increased, the hem reaching to just above the ankles. There were two hip pockets with flaps as on the conventional greatcoat, but also two vertical "muff" pockets placed above them in the torso. Loops and buttons for the attachment of shoulder straps were provided; and the sleeves had the regular French cuff.

The collar of the pre-war model was faced in dark green badge cloth, but this was later changed to field-grey; a buttoning tab underneath allowed it to be turned up and secured around the bottom of the face. At the rear of the collar was a horizontal opening which concealed a rolled hood made from four panels of field-grey drill material similar to that used in tunic and coat linings. When the hood was rolled inside the collar it was held in place by a centrally placed vertical tab and single button. A half-belt at the rear waist was secured by two buttons; the vertical skirt vent below this was closed by four buttons. The watchcoat was entirely lined with either grey or black blanket material; there was a pocket inside the left breast; and a small tab at the left waist buttoned across to secure the right front panel. The pocket of this example is stamped with the size, the manufacturer's name "R.Schmidt", and the depot code for Erfurt, 1939. The sleeves had an insulating interlining beneath the outer lining in field-grey drill.

Winter boots would be made in two patterns, the later design being worn as a boot in itself rather than over the

marching boots like the first pattern illustrated here. This earlier type was provided for soldiers on static duties such as sentries. They were made with a shaft of compressed felt atop a large leather shoe with high sides. There was an opening at the front, covered with a leather storm fly and secured by two horizontal straps. The top and the rear spine were also reinforced with leather strips, and the wooden soles were about 5cm thick for insulation purposes.

The knitted gloves worn here are the standard issue Army pattern in field grey wool. These gloves came in four sizes - small, medium, large and extra large - indicated by the number of knitted-in white rings around the wrists, from one (small) to four (extra large). The headscarf (*Toque*) was a versatile and popular item, tucking well down into the collar and protecting the neck and ears; a plain knitted grey wool tube, it could be worn adjusted at will as a neckscarf or a balaclava, and fitted underneath helmets and most other headgear.

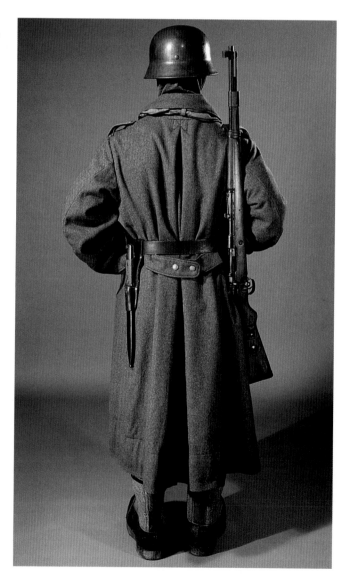

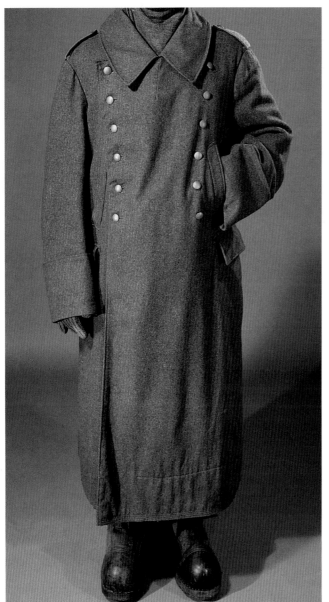

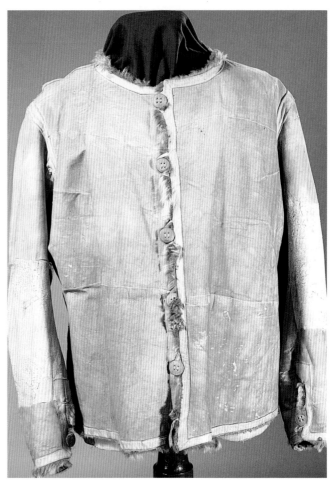

Left
The extra girth and length of the watchcoat is visible here. Note the horizontal seam near the bottom edge of the skirt, which shows the limit of the blanket lining.

Above
Fur jackets such as this were manufactured locally to supplement issue clothing and the publicly donated civilian winter garments which trickled up to the front line from Germany. This jacket is made from rabbit fur with wooden buttons; others were made in a sleeveless vest pattern. Such field-expedient items were normally worn under the coat.

Left
The lining, of a sturdy blanket-type material, will be seen in both field-grey and black; it covers the entire inside of the coat, and the light drab drill material used for the sleeve linings covers an intermediate insulating layer. Note also the left breast pocket; and the buttoning tab used to anchor the right, inner panel of the double-breasted closure.

Above left
The grey knitted gloves and the tube-shaped toque or headscarf. This pair of gloves are identified as medium size by the two white rings.

Above
This pattern of overboot - one shown here with an officer's leather boot inside, in the manner employed - were intended for sentries and others forced to carry out static duties, but of necessity they were sometimes worn on the move. Note the construction of felt and leather, with a deep wooden sole.

Left
A special feature of the watchcoat was the integral hood, rolled and stowed inside the collar when not in use; note, however, that it is only made from a single layer of drill fabric, and thus cannot have offered much protection. The field-grey shoulder straps are piped with Artillery red *Waffenfarbe*.

(14) Field Police enlisted man, motorcycle dress, Southern Russia 1942-44

The Army Field Police (*Feldgendarmerie des Heeres*) were formed at the time of German mobilisation in 1939. The Army recruited experienced police officers from the civil *Gendarmerie*, particularly the motorised branch, and these formed the cadre together with suitable serving Army NCOs. A battalion of *Feldgendarmerie* was subordinated to each field army, and a troop to each division; these units were notably "NCO-heavy" - a troop might have three officers, 41 NCOs and 20 men. All units were motorised and equipped with motorcycles, motorcycle combinations, light and heavy field cars and trucks; they carried small arms and machine guns. Their responsibilities were as widespread as their authority. They directed and controlled traffic, checked the papers of troops in transit, collected documents and intelligence from prisoners, conducted anti-partisan operations, apprehended deserters, and generally maintained order and discipline. The *Feldgendarmerie* had total authority to pass unchallenged through guard posts and secure areas, and to demand the papers of any soldier, regardless of rank.

They wore the same uniform as the rest of the Army, being distinguished by orange *Waffenfarbe* and a special left sleeve badge and cuff-title on the tunic. Their most distinctive adornment, however, was the *Feldgendarmerie* duty gorget (*Ringkragen*); this badge of office showed the wearer to be on duty and endowed with the consequent authority. Its chain suspension gave rise to the soldiers' derogatory nickname for the Field Policeman: "*Kettenhund*" or "chained dog".

The motorcyclist's coat (*Kradmantel*) is more commonly seen in its waterproof version, made of a heavy rubberised cloth in field-grey or field-green with a cloth-faced collar. That illustrated is a lighter weight version made from olive-coloured canvas drill, as used in Africa, southern Europe and southern Russia. The deeply double-breasted coat had an external partial waist belt with three buttonholes in the tip, which ran from the left hip across the back to the right hip, where it engaged with one of three horizontally placed buttons according to size adjustment. At the waist both left and right front edges had a single-button tab for closure. The outermost (left) panel attached to the same right hip buttons as the waist belt, while the innermost (right) panel fastened to a three-button tab set inside the left hip. The top of both panels had two regular buttonholes which allowed both flaps to be closed to the neck like the greatcoat.

Buttonholes in the bottom corners of the skirt at front and rear could be buttoned to the outside lower legs and the inside thighs to form the skirt into separate "legs" in a sort of coverall configuration, convenient and protective when riding astride the motocycle. The ends of the sleeves were gathered into cuffs closed by adjustable two-button tabs. This not uncomplicated system allowed the coat to be sealed around the rider for maximum protection. There was a deep cape across the back of the shoulders which concealed a horizontal vent; this was covered inside with an "Aertex"-type material for ventilation purposes. A large pocket with a vertical forward-buttoning flap was provided at each hip, and a vertical slash pocket in the right breast. The collar on the tropical-weight motorcyclist's coat was of the same material as the body (that of the rubberised waterproof version was field-grey from 1934 to 1935, then of dark green

badge cloth until 1940, when it was changed to the basic field-grey tunic material). Bridles and buttons for the attachment of shoulder straps were provided (the only insignia applied to the coat), those illustrated being field-grey piped with orange *Waffenfarbe*.

The *Feldgendarmerie* duty gorget was designed to be highly visible, even at night in vehicle headlights. The crescent plate was made of stamped steel (later patterns being in a lighter metal). The centre bore the Army pattern spread eagle above a grey-painted scroll bearing the legend "*Feldgendarmerie*", with a pin-back pebbled-finish button at each top corner. The buttons, eagle, and scroll lettering were all finished in a lemon-yellow luminous paint, which allowed Field Police to be identified easily in the dark. The link suspension chain was approximately 24 inches long and made of light metal; it was riveted at one end, the other end hooking to a 2-inch metal prong. An identical vertical prong in the centre back of the plate could be engaged with a tunic buttonhole to hold the gorget steady on the chest. The gorget was backed with either field-grey material or a brittle brown cardboard.

On the standard Army belt this soldier wears a pair of triple pouches for the 32-round magazines of his MP40 machine pistol; he has an issue torch attached to a front coat button, and is controlling traffic with a directing baton.

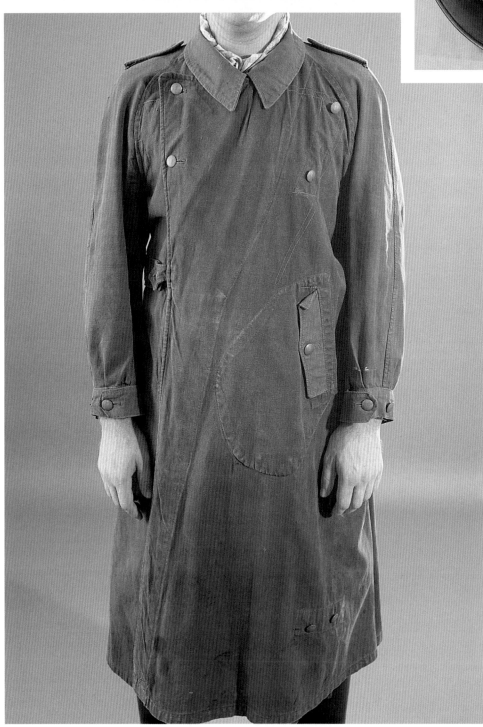

Above left and above
The M35 pattern helmet now has a field-green rather than grey paint finish; only the eagle shield transfer is applied, the tricolour shield being abolished from 1940 as dangerously visible for field use. The liner is the standard M31 pattern; as was common, the owner has painted his name and serial number around the back flange.

Left
The motorcyclist's coat was loosely cut, in both heavy rubberised and lightweight versions, to enable belt equipment to be worn underneath, although in practice this was rarely done. Note the hip pockets, the sleeve cuffs, the single-button tab at the right waist, and the buttons on the lower skirt for securing it around the legs.

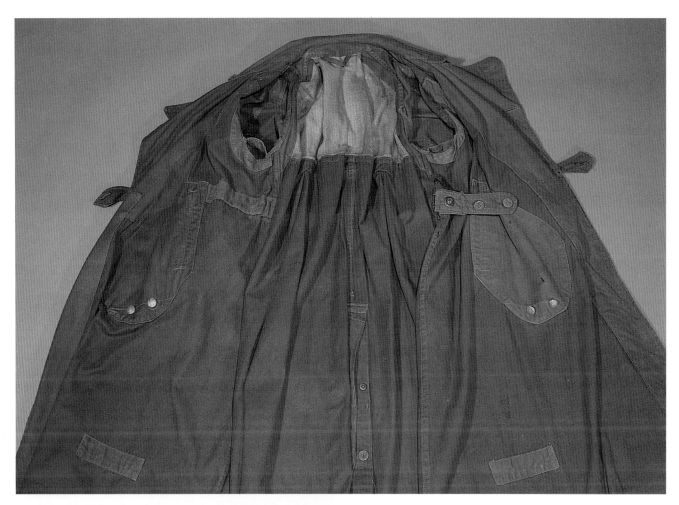

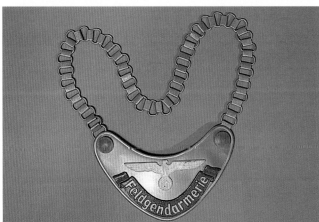

Above
The interior of the coat; light grey "Aertex"-type material at the shoulders provided ventilation, as did vents at the armpits. Note the three-button tab for securing the right panel of the double-breasted front, the single-button tabs at the waist, and the inside buttons for securing the skirt.

Left
This later example of the duty gorget is made from stamped light metal and has a cardboard backing. Note the lemon-yellow luminous paint on the lettering, buttons and eagle.

Bottom left
Paired set of triple magazine pouches for the MP38/MP40 series of 9mm machine pistols (the so-called "Schmeisser"), in unissued condition. Note the belt loops set at a slant, the D-rings on short straps for attachment to the belt support braces, and the extra pocket for the magazine loading tool on the pouches worn on the left side. The belt loops are stamped in this case "clg 43" with the Waffenamt proof stamp, and "MP38 u. 40".

(15) Anti-tank Artillery enlisted man, tropical combat dress, North Africa 1943

The first troops of the German Africa Corps (*Deutsches Afrikakorps or DAK*) arrived in Libya in February 1941 under *Generalleutnant* Erwin Rommel. By the time the greatly expanded *Panzerarmee Afrika* surrendered to large Anglo-American forces in Tunisia in May 1943 a military legend had been born. Germany had only limited historical experience of tropical fighting, and almost every aspect of military equipment and practice had to be adapted to the new environment. A new tropical field service uniform (*Tropenanzug*) was developed in 1940 by the Hamburg Tropical Institute; time and field experience would see some items discarded and others modified. It is worn here as by a veteran *Gefreiter* (senior Private or junior Corporal) of one of the anti-tank units (*Panzerabwehreinheiten*) which played an important part in the campaign, equipped for forward duty in an observation post.

The tropical tunic was styled after the regular service tunic, but with an open collar. It was manufactured from a hard-wearing cotton twill, initially olive in colour but in some later cases a chocolate brown; prolonged wear and washing produced many differing shades. Tunics from 1941 and early 1942 have pleated pockets with scalloped flaps; the pleats disappeared from late 1942 and the flaps became square from early 1943. There were five (occasionally four) olive-painted pebbled-finish front buttons; these and the pocket buttons were not sewn to the tunic, but secured by S-shaped wire split rings. There was no lining, just a cotton reinforcement under the armpits; a medical dressing pocket was provided inside the bottom corner of the right front panel, and one belt support hook at each hip. The sleeves had the usual vent, closed with a pressed paper button.

The insignia were in the same configuration as those of the European service uniform; however, the breast eagle, cap eagle and collar *Litzen* were woven in a light blue-grey thread on a dark sand or mustard-coloured base. *Tresse* braid, for the sleeve chevrons of enlisted ranks and the collars and shoulder straps of NCO ranks, was produced in a copper-brown thread instead of silver or grey. The shoulder straps and tunics left the factory as a matching set, but due to issue of replacement tunics and movement of troops through various branches, it is common for the straps not to match the tunic. Shoulder straps for enlisted and NCO grades were of the slip-on type, lined on the underside with field-grey woollen material. Due to shortages there was extensive use of European items of insignia, and combinations of these and tropical pieces can be encountered. Officers were issued the same tunic as the men and it was up to the individual to substitute European insignia. Some relied only on the shoulder straps to carry their rank, retaining the enlisted-style breast eagle and collar *Litzen*; others wore full officer distinctions, and many combinations will be found.

The breeches were manufactured of either the same material as the tunic or a heavily ribbed cotton twill. They featured two hip pockets and one rear, a fob pocket and retaining ring, with an internal cloth belt and three-clawed buckle at the front closure, belt loops and suspender buttons. The breeches were flared jodhpur-fashion at the thigh, and had vents at the bottom with laces for closure; dished metal buttons were used throughout. Shorts were worn in rear areas, and baggy straight-cut trousers were also extensively worn, usually gathered at the ankle.

Various types of headdress were issued in the African theatre; the rational but impractical sun helmet was initially general issue, but proved quite unpopular. A tropical version of the M34 field cap was issued; this was light and unencumbering, but gave no protection from the sun. The most popular cap, which became a symbol of the *Afrikakorps*, was the peaked field cap based on the shape of the mountain troops' *Bergmütze*, which in turn became the model for the M43 *Einheitsfeldmütze*. Basically an M34 cap with a peak, it was manufactured (like the tropical version of the M34) in the same olive cotton drill as the tunic, with a scarlet lining. The cap carried the national eagle, the flat-woven cockade on a diamond-shaped backing of dark mustard cloth, and (until an order of September 1942) the conventional soutache of "Russia braid" in the appropriate *Waffenfarbe*. For tropical use the *Stahlhelm* was usually painted with sand-coloured vehicle paint, sometimes with sand mixed in to matt the surface still further.

Special tropical boots of olive canvas and brown leather gave a fair degree of protection, but the original calf-length issue were unpopular because of the complicated lacing. This led to the adoption of an ankle-high version which proved acceptable.

Left
The tropical field cap (Tropische Einhheits-feldmütze), made of thin but hard-wearing olive cotton drill with a bright red cotton lining. Note the colours of the standard tropical insignia; and the Russia braid soutache, here in the light blue of Supply troops. It is marked inside to "Franz Richter & Sohne 1942".

Below left
The tropical field blouse (Tropische Feldbluse), of 1943 pattern without scalloped flaps or box pleats on the pockets. The skirt has been shortened, which was a fashion of the day. The single chevron of copper-brown braid on an olive triangular background, worn on the upper left sleeve, is the rank badge of a *Gefreiter*. Note the ribbed twill of the breeches.

Below
The tropical insignia. The "*Afrikakorps*" cuff-title was introduced in July 1941 as a formation distinction; it was still to be seen in 1943, worn by long-service veterans, despite being officially superseded by the "*Afrika* with palms" cuff-title awarded as a campaign decoration in January that year. Note the light grey and mustard-coloured machine-woven collar and breast insignia; and the field-grey underside of the olive canvas shoulder straps, piped in rose-pink for anti-tank units.

Right
Tropical field equipment. The bayonet frog, belt and buckle tab are of olive web - more practical than leather, which deteriorates in extreme heat. The MP40 ammunition pouches are web with leather fittings, stamped "Gustav Reinhardt Berlin 1940". The waterbottle (Feldflasche) is made from a plastic-impregnated wood which did not require a cover.

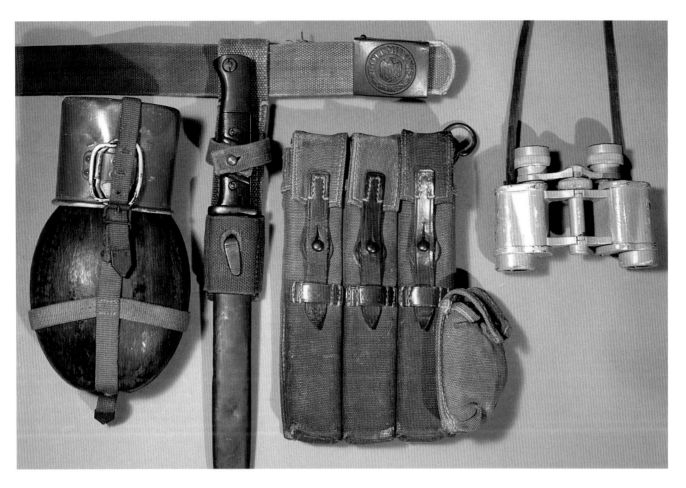

Above
Issue stampings. In early
1943 the revealing depot
stampings were replaced by
a coded number system.
This tunic (upper) carries
the state manufacturing
number (*Reichsbetrieb-
nummer*) RB Nr 0/0774/000.
The breeches (lower)
display size stampings only.
Note the S-shaped wire ring
retaining the tunic button.

Right
The original high tropical
boots, the first of their kind
among the world's armies.
The time-consuming lacing
made them unpopular.The
tropical boots, in both calf-
and ankle-length versions,
will be found both with
and without hobnails.

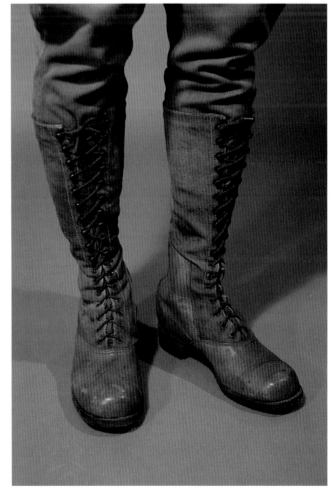

(16) Artillery enlisted man, summer combat dress, Russia 1943-44

The first months of 1943 came to be seen as a turning point for the German *Wehrmacht*. The disaster at Stalingrad cost Germany some 200,000 dead and captured, and four months later about 240,000 men surrendered in Tunisia. German troops were fighting in freezing cold and in blazing summer heat, and units increasingly found themselves rushed between distant fronts to meet sudden emergencies. Various items of uniform suffered from economic cutbacks during the war, but a constant drive towards research and development of new items reflected a concern that the troops should have the best uniforms and equipment possible. The wearing of the reed-green drill fatigue uniform, with the addition of insignia, as a hot weather combat dress was recognised as a practical use of the resources at hand; and led to the introduction of the purpose-made reed-green field service uniform (*Schilfgrüner Drillich Felddienstanzug*). This light, durable outfit was particularly popular as a replacement for the field-grey wool uniform on the hot southern fronts in Russia and the Mediterranean.

This reed-green uniform was introduced as the new summer field service dress at the outset of 1943. The tunic was cut along the lines of the temperate service dress, and was to replace the 1940 reed-green drill uniform, which only had lower pockets. The new tunic was intended to be worn with all service insignia, unlike the previous pattern. The cloth used for this uniform was cotton with a herringbone weave, and will be encountered in a variety of shades from a sea-green to light grey. There were four patch pockets, the flaps having initially a slight scallop but later being cut straight. Down the front six standard buttons were attached by S-rings, which also secured the pocket buttons. There were three buttons for the collar liner, and two in each cuff vent, all made of pressed cardboard. The jacket was only lined in the areas of the cuff vents, armpits, and belt support hook suspension; the material used was initially grey cotton, soon replaced with grey rayon.

The standard mid-war breast eagle is worn, machine-woven in mouse-grey on green. The shoulder straps in basic cloth are seen here with red *Waffenfarbe* for the Artillery. The collar patches in this case are non-regulation - the pre-November 1938 pattern *Litzen* with "lights" in the branch *Waffenfarbe* (minor personal affectations like this will be encountered on many types of uniform clothing from time to time). On the lower left sleeve this soldier wears the Gunner's Proficiency Badge (*Richtkanonier-Abzeichen*) introduced in December 1936. Above the left breast pocket he displays the bronze grade of the Close Combat Clasp (*Nahkampfspange*), introduced in November 1942 to honour troops who had fought in prolonged close combat with small arms only. On the pocket is pinned the 1939 *Verwundeten-Abzeichen* in black: if it marks two wounds already suffered, this gunner - being sent back down the line after first aid, labelled with details of his injury and the medication already administered - has just qualified for the silver grade (three and four wounds).

The new trousers for this uniform were identical to the preceding drill trousers; they were cut similarly to the early service trousers, high at the back, with a straight leg. There were two slash pockets at the hips, and a small patch fob pocket at the right groin. There was no lining, and the rear waist had a horizontal adjustment tab for fit. Metal washer buttons were used throughout.

The steel helmet M42 (*Stahlhelm-Modell 1942*) was introduced in April 1942 as an economy measure; the sizes and shape of the M35 were retained, but the outer edge was no longer crimped under, being simply flared outwards and sheared. The left side transfer of the armed forces eagle (*Wehrmachts-Adler*) was officially used until August 1943; but this example of the helmet displays a field re-paint of dark green with faint lighter green camouflage spots. Such field-painted finishes will be frequently encountered, and were used in all theatres of combat.

This gunner wears the now-standard laced ankle boots with hobnails and canvas anklet gaiters (*Gamaschen*). Although the ankle boot (*Schnürschuhe*) began to be introduced in August 1940 to conserve stocks of leather, the troops clung jealously to the leather marching boot, and avoided use of the gaiters for as long as possible. The issue belt and P08 pistol holster are worn here, gunners being issued a personal sidearm for protection in the gun area.

Right
The M42 steel helmet, identifiable by its sharp, uncrimped rim.
This helmet displays one of a wide variety of field-applied paint finishes; as well as spotted camouflage overlay (hardly apparent in the photos, but clearly discernible on the piece) it has sand mixed into the paint to give a dull finish.

Below
The reed-green tunic; its general conformity to the service tunic cut can be seen here. While the collar buttons to the top, it was normally worn unbuttoned. Note the Close Combat Clasp on the left breast, and the Gunner's Proficiency Badge on the left forearm.

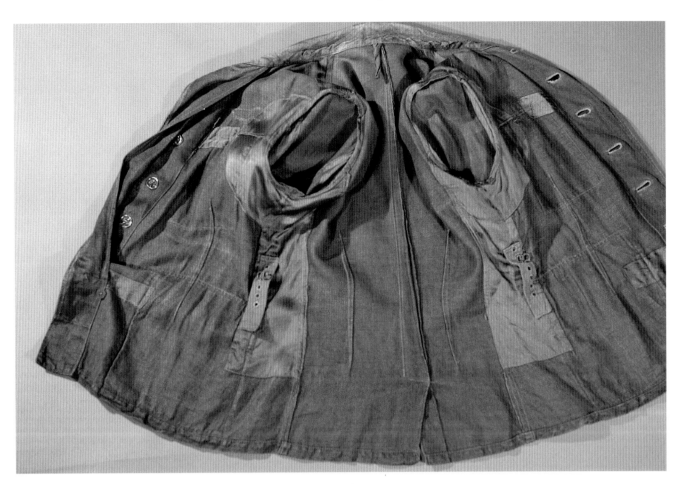

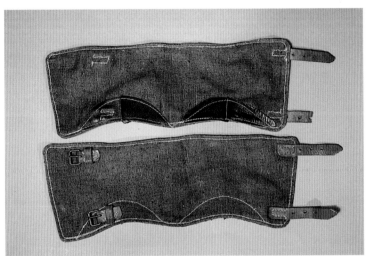

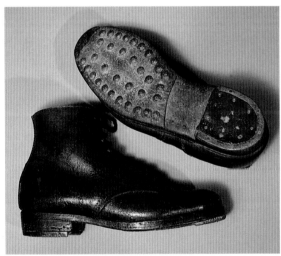

Left
The shoulder straps are in field-grey woollen material with Artillery Waffenfarbe, and the mid-war breast eagle is in mouse-grey on green (later versions had field-grey backing). The regulation "subdued" field service collar Litzen have been removed and replaced with the type officially discarded in 1938, complete with strips of Waffenfarbe.

Top
The simplified tunic lining, in the later grey rayon material. Note the two belt support hook suspension tabs, and the buttons attached with S-rings.

Above left
Though lighter, the canvas gaiters closely resembled the British "anklets, web" and were almost certainly a direct copy; they were highly unpopular. Both black and brown leather were used in their manufacture, and all-canvas examples will occasionally be found.

Above
This pair of standard issue ankle boots display the typical pattern of hobnails; note also note the metal plates at heel and toe.

(17) Artillery NCO, summer dress, Italy 1943-44

Despite the fact that the German Army was locked in a war of national survival, across many fronts, the importance of wearing smart uniforms and insignia was not lost on either the troops or the High Command. (It has been said that German soldiers went into battle as if going on parade; British soldiers, as if to a sporting event; and American soldiers, as if going to work.) Apart from merely distinguishing friend from foe, distinctive uniform and insignia represented a symbol of authority, visibly bound the wearer to his comrades in a common cause, identified branch of service and rank, and contributed to *esprit de corps*.

During the war tailored lightweight service tunics became very popular among German officers and NCOs; though strictly non-regulation, they were tolerated as being practical while not detracting from a proper military appearance. These jackets were usually produced from lightweight drill material and were seen in a variety of shades, from light grey to reed-green and sandy beige. While the tunics almost always featured the old-style dark green collar and a full set of insignia, the canvas material gave a "field" look which was appealing.

This *Oberfeldwebel* (Sergeant-Major) wears a tunic patterned after the wool service tunic but with several minor alterations. It has been cut from a lightweight drill material, originally of a pale grey-green colour but now bleached to a sandy shade by the sun. There are four patch pockets with pleats and straight flaps. The five front and four pocket buttons are of the field-grey pebbled-finish type. Like many similar examples the tunic has a pointed dark green collar, closed by two hooks. The cuffs are plain and lack the usual rear adjustment vent. The back panels of the tunic are finished with "old style" seams arcing down from the shoulders to the small of the back.

The shoulder straps of rank are piped in red Artillery *Waffenfarbe*; it is interesting to note that as the owner has been promoted the straps have been up-graded, the *Tresse* across the end of the strap (and presumably the rank stars) being added to what were once *Unteroffizier's* straps. The collar is edged with *Tresse*, and bears 1935 pattern *Litzen* with *Waffenfarbe* and dark green backing. The breast eagle is a superior hand-embroidered piece employing heavy bullion thread, and is sewn on by hand with heavy stitches; such officer-grade eagles were quite common on NCO's tailored lightweight tunics.

This *Oberfeldwebel* wears the ribbon for the Iron Cross 2nd Class from the second buttonhole to the edge of the tunic, the pin-back Iron Cross 1st Class, and a ribbon bar for the Eastern Winter Campaign 1941-42 medal. At the throat he wears an interesting "field" version of the Knight's Cross of the Iron Cross. These were occasionally made by modifying the suspension ring on a 2nd Class Iron Cross; if this was flat to the medal the Knight's Cross suspension loop and neck ribbon could be used. While the Iron Cross was 7mm smaller than the Knight's Cross on each side, the appearance was close; the replacement for this most prestigious of awards could be displayed in the field rather than endangering the real *Ritterkreuz*.

The breeches are the pattern for wear by mounted troops, and are probably worn more as a status symbol than for practical reasons by this senior NCO off duty behind the lines. They are the standard pattern with the seat reinforced with doubled cloth rather than leather, and in this case are stamped "E 40" for Erfurt 1940 (see section 11 for a full description).

Another status symbol favoured by senior NCOs was the peaked *Schirmmütze* of the pattern for non-commissioned and enlisted ranks. This example, with Artillery *Waffenfarbe* piping and stamped light metal insignia, is entirely conventional, though the Sergeant-Major has followed the widespread fashion for removing the wire stiffener and crushing the sides of the cap down to achieve a "front line" look.

Left
This standard issue peaked cap for non-commissioned and enlisted ranks, with red Artillery piping, has had the crown stiffening removed. The lining is of the rust-brown waterproof fabric found in most issue enlisted men's caps.

Below left
This non-regulation privately tailored lightweight tunic closely follows the pattern of the service tunic. Note the straight cuffs and the pointed collar.

Below
Details of the 1935-38 pattern collar Litzen; collar Tresse; and hand-embroidered officer-style breast eagle in heavy bullion thread. Note the retrospective addition of Tresse across the outer end of the shoulder strap, suggesting that the rank insignia have been up-graded on what were originally Unteroffizier's straps. The original colour of the tunic cloth is visible under the pocket flap.

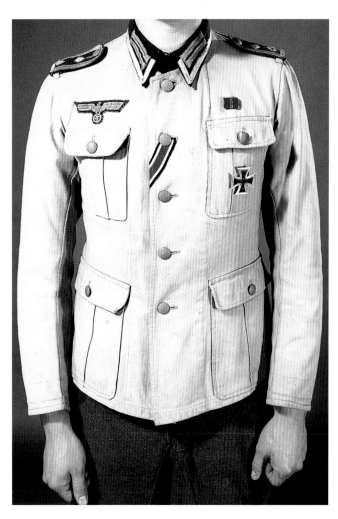

Top
This tunic is completely unlined, and lacks buttons for a collar liner. The original pale grey-green colour of the material is seen inside, contrasting with faded areas around the edges.

Right
Details of the breeches; manufactured in 1940, they already have doubled cloth seat reinforcement rather than leather.

Above
"Replacement Knight's Cross" - an Iron Cross 2nd Class with the suspension ring modified to accept the ribbon clip of the Knight's Cross, allowing it to be worn as a field substitute for the precious higher award.

(18) Mountain Rifles enlisted man, combat dress, Russia 1943-44

At the start of the war Germany was able to field three full divisions of Mountain Troops (*Gebirgstruppen*). The concept of troops trained and equipped specifically for operations in mountainous areas dated from before World War I and was tested in battle during that conflict, when German, Austrian and Italian mountain formations had contested the Alpine front. The nature of their mission required *Gebirgsjäger* (Mountain Rifles, as the infantry element were traditionally titled) to be fit, highly trained, and self-reliant; the bulk of recruits were drawn from the mountain regions of southern Germany and Austria. They fought in Poland and in Norway; were air-landed on Crete; fought in Lappland on the Arctic Circle, in the Balkans, in the Caucasus, and in Italy. Within the Mountain Divisions the Rifle regiments were supported by integral Artillery, Signals, Engineer, Anti-tank, and other supporting units, all nominally mountain-qualified.

The field service uniform model 1943 (*Dienstanzug Modell 1943*) was introduced for all types of unmounted Army units in that year to replace all previous models. The new tunic showed evidence of several economy measures. The patch pockets were without pleats; and while early examples had the scalloped pocket flaps, these were soon replaced by plain straight flaps. Due to the inferior quality of the fabric now being used the front closure had six buttons instead of the previous five. The lining was now usually made from a bronze-brown shade of rayon.

The collar patches are second-pattern *Einheitslitzen*, which retain the backing patch; but the third pattern, without the backing, will often be encountered on these tunics. The shoulder straps should be the field-grey type by this date, but examples of the dark green pattern continued to be worn until the end of the war. These straps have field-grey backing and the tongues lined with rayon (artificial satin); they are piped in the light green *Waffenfarbe* of the Mountain Rifles. The breast eagle is the standard wartime type in mouse-grey on field grey. The rank chevron on the left sleeve is the 1943 pattern for an *Obergefreiter* (Corporal) with less than six years service (note the black thread border to the *Tresse* braid). The specialist badge worn above the rank chevron is for Signals personnel (*Nachrichtenpersonal*), the lightning flash being embroidered in the individual's appropriate *Waffenfarbe* - here, Mountain green - on a dark green oval patch. The edelweiss right sleeve badge distinguished all categories of Mountain Troops of all ranks, and was introduced in May 1939. The badge consisted of an edelweiss flower surrounded by a rope border and crowned with a climbing piton; it is found both hand-embroidered in wool and machine-woven in cotton.

The model 1943 field trousers saw the introduction of a more practical design for wear in the field. As well as the usual buttons for attaching braces (suspenders) they were provided with four belt loops; this allowed the trousers to be lowered without also removing the tunic and belt equipment. The legs were tapered to the ankle for wearing with ankle boots and gaiters, with an adjustable vent and tapes. There were three slash pockets and a watch fob pocket, all of them with buttons; this example uses dished metal buttons throughout, although resin buttons may be encountered. An adjustment tab was fitted to each hip at the waist, and a reinforcing patch was sewn over the seat and crutch. Some models had an internal waistbelt and buckle.

The field cap model 1943 (*Einheitsfeldmütze M43*) which was introduced with this uniform proved to be the most popular and practical cap of the war. The pattern resembled both the *Bergmütze* and the tropical field cap. The peak - stiffened internally with cardboard, and often worn with a folded crease down the middle - was long enough to shade and protect the eyes. The flap around the body, secured by two small pebbled-finish buttons, could be unfolded and lowered around the ears and chin for warmth. Early-manufacture caps were lined with a heavy cotton drill. Insignia consisted of the mouse-grey national eagle and tricolour cockade machine-woven on a single backing patch of truncated triangular shape. The M43 cap replaced the earlier *Bergmütze* (similar, but with a shorter peak) among Mountain Troops; the metal edelweiss badge to which all ranks of that branch were entitled is worn here on the left side.

The standard mountain boots are worn, with short puttees which gave ankle support and kept snow and dirt out of the boots. The standard belt order is worn but without supporting braces, as these are an integral part of the M31 mountain rucksack shown here.

Above left & above
Although many soldiers retained the boat-shaped M34 field cap for varying periods, the M43 Einheitsfeldmütze ("universal issue field cap") which replaced it from 1943 proved to be the most popular field headgear of the war, being worn by every type of unit and by all ranks from General to Private. Note the one-piece machine-woven insignia; the metal edelweiss tradition badge of the Mountain Troops sewn to the left side of this example; and the lining in grey cotton drill, soon to be replaced by artificial satin. There are faint manufacturer's markings, "Mützenfabrik" and "1943".

Left
The M43 tunic is worn here with the collar open, although it could still be buttoned to the neck. Note the declining quality of the cloth, which now requires a six-button closure; and the front belt support hooks, protruding through hemmed eyelets.

Above
This tunic exemplifies the common mixed use of both early-pattern and wartime-pattern insignia on the same garment; individuals would receive or replace insignia at different dates, and unless a complete replacement outfit was drawn a miscellany of patterns was inevitable.

Above left
The windjacket (Windjacke für Gebirgstruppen) provided only to Mountain Troops. This example has the edelweiss badge added, with the backing cut away - a personal, non-regulation touch - and has also had the shoulder strap attachments removed. Of strong, waterproof cotton duck material, it has two skirt pockets and two "muff" pockets. The collar and cuffs could be closed tightly, and large resin or dished metal buttons were used throughout.

Left
The interior of the tunic, showing the rayon (artificial satin) lining and the four belt support hook tabs. Also shown are the 1943 field trousers, with buttoning belt loops and legs tapered to the ankle, which features a vent closed by a drawstring.

(19) Mountain Rifles officer, summer dress, Italy 1943-44

In late 1943 the *Wehrmacht* was heavily engaged against the British 8th Army, US 5th Army and other Allied troops on the Italian mainland. The difficult, mountainous terrain favoured the skillful defensive campaign conducted by *Generalfeldmarschall* Kesselring, in which the Army's Mountain Troops and the *Luftwaffe* Parachute Divisions played leading parts. The climate on the Italian front varied from the severest of winter conditions to near-tropical temperatures, and this was reflected in the curious mixture of uniform items worn by the troops. Combat dress was, by now, governed by purely practical choices, and in hot weather there was a proliferation of shorts, lightweight trousers, ankle boots, loose-fitting tunics and soft caps.

This particular tunic was reputedly made for the invasion of Crete, but this has not been confirmed. The cut is the same as that of the service tunic. It has four pleated patch pockets with scalloped flaps, and five front buttons. The material used is a light, ribbed cotton, which was originally a light grey but has been bleached by the sun to the sandy shade seen here. The sleeves are finished with turned-back cuffs, and the tunic skirt is cut fashionably short. Like most lightweight tunics this example has only a half-lining, running across the shoulders and the upper part of the chest. (Curiously, however, a vent has been provided for carriage of the dress dagger or sabre.)

The *Oberleutnant's* shoulder straps are of the dull silver "field" type, with underlay in the green *Waffenfarbe* for Mountain Troops. The collar *Litzen*, while of high quality hand-embroidered pattern, are unusual in lacking "lights" of *Waffenfarbe* centred on the bars; the breast eagle is hand-embroidered in heavy bullion thread. The Mountain Troops' edelweiss right sleeve badge differs from the enlisted ranks' pattern only in having a silver-embroidered piton (instead of light grey) at the top centre. This officer displays three awards: the ribbon for the Iron Cross 2nd Class, the General Assault Badge, and the silver Close Combat Clasp. Interestingly, the broad, irregularly shaped attachment pin for the Clasp requires asymmetric sewn loops, the left larger than the right, and these are present.

Our figure wears the new cloth trousers (*Tuchhose*) which were introduced in June 1943 to replace all previous long trousers. These trousers had a straight waistband, with four buttoning belt loops and an adjustment tab at each hip. While some examples had an internal belt and buckle fitted at the waist, many were manufactured without it. There were two hip and one rear buttoning slash pockets, and a small fob pocket with flap at the right groin. The leg was no longer straight, but tapered for wear with gaiters or puttees and ankle boots; and the seat was reinforced with an oval-shaped doubled cloth patch. There were cloth laces at the foot to form an adjustable "stirrup" for a securer fit.

This *Oberleutnant* wears the mountain troop's cap (*Bergmütze*). This cap, a distinction of the *Gebirgsjäger* from the earliest days of the war, was later the inspiration for the popular M43 "universal issue field cap". The mountain cap consisted of a soft crown which was stiffened at the front, and a short cloth-covered peak. The broad fold-up curtain or flap around the front and sides could be lowered over the ears and chin in bad weather; it was initially fastened by two

opaque glass buttons, but these were later replaced by conventional pebbled-finish buttons. The lining was made from grey cotton or ribbed cotton drill material, with a sweatband of either thin grey leather or a cardboard-based leatherette. The cap badge took the form of the national eagle over the cockade in national colours, machine-woven on a single T-shaped dark green backing; the officer's badge had the eagle and the "white" cockade ring woven in silver thread. Officers were not ordered to wear silver piping around the crown seam of the cap until October 1942; most officers' caps encountered will therefore show evidence of this piping being retrospectively fitted. All ranks of the *Gebirgstruppen* wore the metal edelweiss tradition badge on the left side of the cap, sewn on at a backwards slant through holes in the tips of the petals and stem.

The mountain boots were constructed of quality brown or black leather with a field-green cloth strip around the top. The heavy sole and heel had patterns of heavy studs in the centre, with metal cleats placed around the outer edges. Small metal plates at the toe, and a bevelled heel, enabled them to be used with skis.

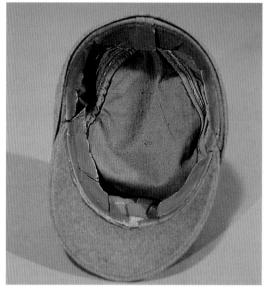

Above left & above
The more rounded crown shape and the short peak - the main features distinguishing the Bergmütze from the later M43 cap - are evident here. Note the T-form of the badge backing, the officer's piping around the crown, and the metal edelweiss tradition badge. The lining is in a heavy ribbed twill material, which is marked only with the size. Note the card sweatband (which has cracked with use); and the white stitching, indicating the retrospective attachment of the silver crown piping in accordance with the order of October 1942.

Left
The copying of the service tunic pattern is apparent here. Note the fashionable features such as the narrow waist, the short skirt and the pointed collar tips.

Above
The epaulettes show the green Waffenfarbe for Mountain Troops, though note that this is absent from the collar patch Litzen; the gold wash is almost worn off the single star of Oberleutnant's rank.

Above right
The crudely made Leuchtpistole 42 was introduced in 1943 to simplify production of the Army flare pistol; it retained the 2.7cm cartridge. The large leather pouch carried 18 flare cartridges; note the label for the pre-war Walther flare pistol, and the proof stamp by its bottom left corner.

Right
These mountain boots are constructed of high quality brown leather, and are fitted with heavy patterns of studs and edge cleats. Note the protective strip of field-green cloth at the top of the ankle.

(20) Infantry enlisted man, reversible winter combat dress, Russia 1942-44

After the disastrous first winter in Russia the Quartermaster-General of the Army was ordered to develop a winter combat uniform for the next winter campaign season. The uniform which resulted was tested in Finland, and in April 1942 was exhibited to Hitler for his approval, which was immediately granted. The textile industry were ordered to produce one million sets in time for the next winter. In winter 1942 the scale of winter clothing issue was increased to include not only the new padded jacket and trousers but also a number of other protective items such as a matching insulated hood and over-mittens, the woollen toque headscarf, gloves (both woollen and fur-lined), extra socks, a pullover, etc. While most troops of all branches of the Army received - in time - the basic uniform, and priority branches, such as the Infantry, these extra items, it was not until winter 1943-44 that the padded uniform could really be termed "general issue". It is clear from photographs, for instance, that it was far from generally available among the troops of the 6th Army which was destroyed at Stalingrad in winter 1942-43.

The new padded, reversible winter suit was initially produced in a mouse-grey colour reversible to white. This was soon superseded (perhaps during late 1942, and certainly by early 1943) by an identical pattern in which the mouse-grey was replaced by printed camouflage patterns - initially the *Splittermuster* or "splinter pattern" already in use on the *Zeltbahn* shelter section, and illustrated in these photographs. During 1943 the camouflage winter uniform (*Wintertarnanzug*) began to appear in the *Sumpfmuster* or "marsh pattern" camouflage, sometimes called by modern collectors "tan water pattern"; it is known in both the greenish-based and beige-based variants of this pattern, and in the less sharply printed so-called "*Sumpfmuster 44*" pattern. The over-mittens and hood were coloured in the same way as the suit. This uniform was popular with the troops and continued to be used until the end of the war.

The *Wintertarnanzug* was constructed at first from the same heavy cotton/rayon material as the *Zeltbahn*, and later from a lighter 100% spun rayon shell, both with inner layers of cellulose wool for insulation. It was generously cut to fit over other clothing and field equipment (though the latter was normally worn over it in practice), and completely reversible; all buttons, pockets, drawstrings, etc., were present and functional on both camouflage and white sides. The jacket was double-breasted and fastened with six buttons down the front, on both obverse and reverse, the buttonholes sewn into a flap of material which formed a fold-over fly. The length was slightly longer than the service tunic; there was a pocket with an external buttoning flap in each hip, and a "tunnel" round the waist for a heavy tape drawstring. The cuffs had tightening tapes which could be adjusted over two buttons. An integral hood, of doubled cloth and with a drawstring round the rim but not insulated, was cut large enough to fit over the helmet. High on the front and rear sleeve seams were set two resin buttons for attachment of coloured temporary identification bands. Standard pebbled-finish buttons were used, painted field-grey on the camouflage side and matt white on the white side.

The reversible trousers were made from the same material as the jacket; cut high at the waist, they had adjustment laces at the rear waist and running round inside the leg bottoms, and integral white fabric suspenders (braces) sewn together where they crossed at the back. They had a pocket at each hip, covered with a buttoning flap; the fly front was closed with three or four large buttons and was covered by an outer buttoning flap. All buttons on the trousers were large and made of resin or plastic, although the standard metal button is occasionally seen.

The trousers illustrated here are an interesting example of a not uncommon variation; they are not reversible to white, but are lined instead with grey artificial satin (rayon). Original examples of both jackets and trousers of this type may be encountered, in camouflage of both *Splittermuster* and *Sumpfmuster* patterns.

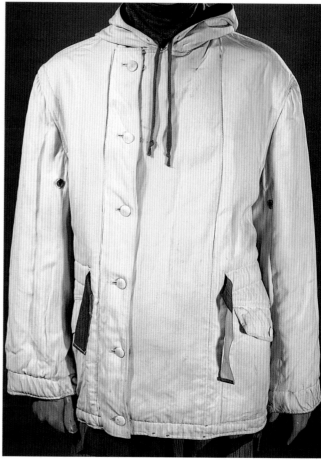

Above left
The camouflage side of the reversible jacket, in the initial Splittermuster 31 pattern. Note the covering fly with the front buttonholes, the drawstring slits at the waist, and the upper sleeve buttons for attaching temporary identification bands in the "colours of the day".

Above
The jacket reversed to the white side for snow camouflage; note that all features of the camouflage-patterned side are duplicated. Before the introduction of the Winteranzug troops fighting in snow had to improvise white ponchos and helmet covers from any suitable material they could find.

Left
An interesting variant example of the trousers of the Wintertarnanzug, this pair printed in Splittermuster 31 but not reversing to white, being lined instead with grey rayon. Examples of such lined, non-reversible winter trousers and jackets printed in either "splinter", "marsh", or "1944 marsh" patterns are not uncommon. Note details of the front fly closure panel, the braces, and the factory-applied knee reinforcement patches.

Opposite top left
A common alternative to the issued camouflage/white over-mittens were these field-green "trigger-finger mittens" with leather reinforcement and wrist straps. Introduced in November 1941, this type have off-white wool lining.

Opposite top right
Protective undergarments. The padded vest seen here is one of many types of semi-official winter undergarments manufactured; it fastens with four washer buttons. The "long john" drawers are regulation issue, marked with an "RB" number; they fasten with beige cardboard buttons.

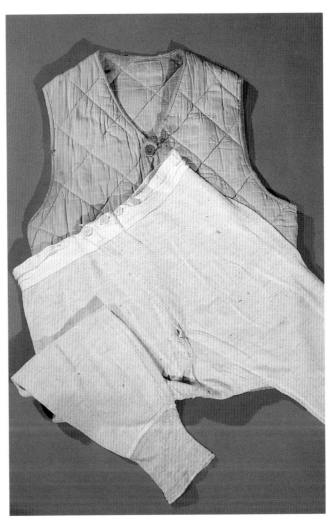

Below
Typical light fighting equipment of the first half of the war - belt order, without the knapsack or gasmask. It consists of the belt; the "belt supports with auxiliary straps", with D-rings and under-arm straps to engage with the backpack when worn; M11 rifle cartridge pouches; S84/98 bayonet in a frog with added hilt strap, the scabbard slipped into the carrier straps of the "small entrenching tool"; the M31 "breadbag", for rations, field stove, and small personal kit, found in canvas of various shades; one of many variants of the basic M31 "field flask" (waterbottle); and the M31 "cook pot" (messtin) set.

(21) Tank Destroyer NCO, combat dress, Russia 1943-44

Originally the Army anti-tank units (*Panzerabwehreinheiten*) were equipped only with towed cannon; as hostilities progressed new weapons and tactics were developed, and a proportion of these units were converted onto self-propelled guns. Initially guns were installed in semi-open mountings on various half- and fully-tracked chassis, modified from both German and captured foreign vehicles. From the mid-war years anti-tank units were increasingly equipped with fully enclosed armoured vehicles - *Panzerjäger* or tank destroyers. Mounting ordnance in low-profile fixed superstructures rather than in traversing turrets, these self-propelled guns were simpler and cheaper to build than conventional tanks, and could perform many defensive tasks equally well.

The concept of the self-propelled assault gun or *Sturmgeschutz* - a cannon mounted in an enclosed armoured vehicle for direct infantry support - dated from the beginning of the war, and in 1940 a new uniform for these SP artillery crews was trialled. It was basically identical to the *Panzertruppe* black vehicle uniform but in field-grey. Initially it had a dark green collar, and included a grey version of the *Schutzmütze* padded beret, but these features were missing from the uniform adopted in January 1941; it also lacked *Waffenfarbe* piping around the collar edge; and - like the black version - it never bore NCO collar *Tresse*. The grey colour probably reflected the practical consideration that crews often had to work outside the vehicles. The field-grey uniform was subsequently issued to the self-propelled *Panzerjäger* units, with a confusing variety of different collar patches, and with rose-pink replacing the red *Waffenfarbe* of the Artillery.

In May 1941 a summer-weight uniform in field-green drill material was introduced for armoured car crews; it proved popular in hot weather, and was soon being issued to the crews of all kinds of AFVs. Among several versions, later patterns featured a large map pocket on the outside left breast. The jacket illustrated is a privately purchased version, closely following the pattern of the first issue drill uniform. It is made from field-green canvas in the classic double-breasted style; the front is secured by three cast-resin buttons concealed by a fly (the issue jacket has four), and by two smaller buttons securing the right front panel to loops inside the left panel. The jacket is unlined, but one pocket is provided inside the left breast. Although there is no corresponding button to allow the neck to be buttoned closed, there is a single buttonhole at the top of the left lapel. This is a cosmetic feature commonly found on tailored *Panzer* jackets, usually serving as the fixing point for medal ribbons - here, those of the War Merit Cross 2nd Class and the medal for the Russian Winter Campaign 1941/42. The sleeves have the usual adjustment vent, here secured by a single resin button.

The shoulder straps for *Feldwebel* (Sergeant-Major) are faced with the same canvas material as the jacket, but with the normal field-grey wool underside; the retaining tongue is lined with artificial satin (rayon). The *Tresse* braid is woven in light grey cotton in "subdued" style. The breast eagle is machine-woven in light grey on mouse-grey backing. The most confusing aspect of the field-grey SP assault artillery and tank destroyer uniform is the variety of collar patches,

prescribed by a bewildering succession of regulations which were often ignored, or superseded before they could be obeyed. *Panzerjäger* units originally wore the standard Army *Doppellitzen* bars; later these were worn with the dark green base outlined in *Waffenfarbe* piping. These were replaced by the black, pink-piped rhomboid-shaped *Panzer* patches complete with death's-heads; and the final pattern was as illustrated - *Litzen* on field-grey outlined with *Waffenfarbe*.

Although most *Panzerjäger* crews were entitled to the General Assault Badge, some personnel were transferred from the tank troops and already had the *Panzerkampfabzeichen*, as illustrated.

The woollen trousers of the vehicle uniform were identical to those of the *Panzer* uniform apart from colour; they are found in a whole range of shades from this light field-grey to the late war olive brown/green material. The cap is the standard M34 *Feldmutze* with pink braid soutache. The laced ankle boots are not hobnailed, to avoid slipping and sparks when clambering around the steel vehicle. The standard issue belt supports a holstered P08 (often retained despite official adoption of the Walther P38). This vehicle commander carries a pair of 8x24 periscope binoculars manufactiured in occupied France; and note the original 20-litre "jerrycan", manufactured in 1941.

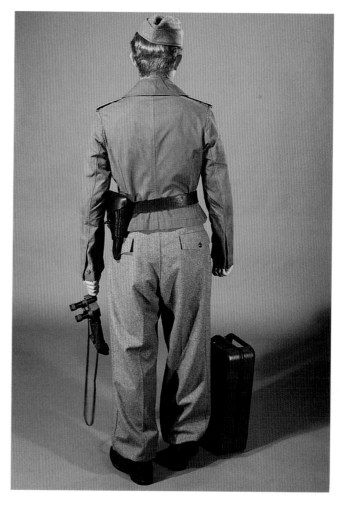

Right
The M34 field cap, popular with armoured vehicle crews, allowed unobstructed use of headphones and vehicle optics. Rose-pink Waffenfarbe was common to both tank and anti-tank troops.

Right
Linings were of cotton drill in various shades from beige to dark grey. Note manufacturer's stamp - K.H.Flauder of Minden, Westfalia, dated 1941. Later caps often had a size marking only.

Bottom left
This privately purchased jacket outwardly copies the pattern of the first issue lightweight drill jacket for armoured crews. It is interesting that individuals went to the trouble of ordering privately tailored versions even of garments destined for hard wear in the front line. In the field a variety of sweaters and turtle-neck tops were tolerated; they were practical and popular.

Opposite top left
The trousers of the vehicle service uniform in field-grey wool, cut to the same practical pattern as those of the black Panzer uniform. Note the forward-buttoning flaps of the pockets, and the button and tape for gathering the ankles.

Opposite top right
The jacket insignia. Note details of the shoulder straps: Feldwebel's rank (light grey cotton Tresse and white metal star); field-green canvas facing on field-grey wool backing, with rayon-lined tongue. These collar patches, worn only on the grey and green vehicle uniforms, are of the last in a confusing series of patterns regulated at various times during the war.

Opposite bottom
Like most summer-weight jackets, this example is unlined; it has no provision for belt support hooks. It has single-button cuff vents, and a single patch pocket in the left breast. Note the buttons and loops on the right and left panels respectively.

90

(22) Major General, service dress, France 1943-44

The general officer corps of the German Army during World War II was an organisation riven with contradictions, and subject to conflicting influences both political and military. While some generals felt that it was their patriotic duty to quietly resist National Socialist influence, others tolerated this, or even profited by it. Hitler tended to distrust the general officer corps, a legacy of both his class background and his service as a ranker in 1914-18.

The basis for the general officer's uniform was the standard officer's service dress, distinguished by the use of gold adornments and insignia and red *Waffenfarbe*. Details vary from uniform to uniform, since virtually all items were tailor-made to individual order, and since generals often availed themselves of a certain latitude (e.g., some general officers displayed red *Waffenfarbe* piping around the tunic collar and down the edge of the front panels, while others did not). The tunic illustrated is of the standard design, a high quality tailored piece with a dark green collar, deep French cuffs, four box-pleated patch pockets with scalloped flaps, and six front buttons (though tunics with eight will be encountered). All buttons are gold-coloured, with the usual pebbled finish. The lining is in a grey satin material with the usual tailored features: an adjustment belt at the waist, a dagger suspender and a vent behind the left pocket, and a vertical slash pocket inside the left breast. The tailor's label at the neck is for "Krüger. Schneider + Herrenausstatter Gau Landeshauptstadt Weimar".

The most distinctive feature of the generals' uniform was the insignia. The shoulder straps were of plaited triple cord in a gold-silver-gold sequence, mounted on an underlay of red. Rank stars and devices were made from German silver: Major Generals wore no stars, Lieutenant Generals one star, Generals two, Colonel Generals three, and General Field Marshals a crossed batons device. The collar patches were of the traditional Prussian pattern called "Larisch embroidery" (*Larisch-Stickerei*), hand-embroidered in gold metallic thread on a red base; the pattern was the same for ranks from Major General to Colonel General, and extended in length for Field Marshals. Some minor colour variations will be encountered, with differing shades of gold thread being used to create highlight effects. The breast eagle was the standard Army pattern, worked in gold thread on a dark green backing. Prior to 1938 the embroidery was done with metallic gold thread which exhibits a very rich, golden colour. After this date a substitute thread called "Cellon" was ordered to be used, and this is recognisable by its relatively paler yellow shade. Many insignia continued to be made in real gold bullion thread after 1938, however, in quiet contravention of the order.

This young divisional commander's awards and decorations are the 1914 Iron Cross 2nd Class ribbon in the second buttonhole, with the added "bar" indicating a subsequent award of the 1939 Iron Cross 2nd Class; the 1939 Iron Cross 1st Class pinned to the pocket, together with the Tank Battle Badge and the Wound Badge in black; and a ribbon bar displaying awards and long service medals for both World Wars and the interwar period.

The general officer's *Schirmmütze* followed the conventional pattern, differing only in the piping, badges and cords fitted.

The usual *Waffenfarbe* was replaced by gold piping; the side buttons and chin cords were also in gold. Prior to January 1943 the eagle and the wreath with cockade were made in silver-coloured metal or embroidery, but after this date all general officers were required to wear gold-coloured badges; this cap has both badges hand-embroidered in gold wire thread. The lining is in a bronze-coloured silk, with the sweatshield marked "Erel Sonderklasse Berlin", as well as "Offizier Kleiderkasse" - this means it was made available through the Officer's Clothing Fund, which provided regulation items to the officer corps. The word "Extra" indicates the highest quality.

The breeches worn by general officers were adorned with the generals' traditional red side-stripes (*Lampassen*). The stone-grey pair worn here carry a label for "Scharnagl & Horr, Mannheim P7.19" behind the rear inside pocket. Generals wore the standard officer's service belt, but with the buckle in a gold colour rather than silver. Note the intricately carved "*Wolchowstock*", a traditional souvenir of the Eastern Front popular amongst German front line officers; it was usually carved for a commander by his men with motifs appropriate to the unit. This example is carved from peachwood, with a flare cartridge as the ferrule.

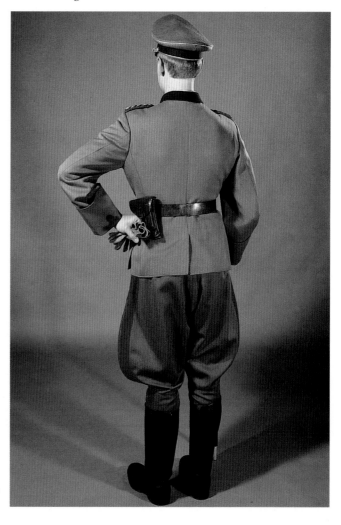

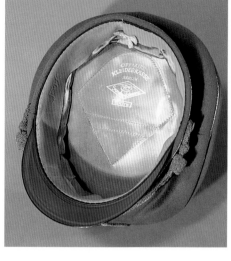

Above left & above
This general officer's Schirmmütze bears the post-1942 badges in gold thread. Note the colour difference between the band and crown piping in synthetic "Cellon", and the gold bullion wire embroidery of the badges. The stampings on the sweatshield protecting the crown lining show that this cap was made by the leading Berlin firm of "Erel" (Robert Lubstein). The markings "Sonderklasse" and "Extra" indicate high quality (and price).

Left
Detail of the Major General's tunic unbelted, showing its superior cut and materials, gold buttons and embroidered insignia.

Opposite top
The grey satin tunic lining displays the common features of a tailor-made piece: an adjustable waist belt, a dagger suspender and clip extending from below the left armpit, and a vent inside the left skirt pocket for the dagger hanger to pass through.

Opposite bottom left
Major General's shoulder strap, collar patch and breast eagle. The shoulder straps seen here are of older manufacture, showing a more bronze-coloured tone than bright gold in the metallic cord; they are also somewhat tarnished with age. There is no indication of branch of service on regulation general officers' shoulder straps of rank. Note the heavy gold wire embroidery used in the collar patches and breast eagle.

Opposite bottom right
These fine quality breeches display the general officer's traditional red Lampassen side-stripes: two 4cm-wide stripes placed 0.5cm each side of a single seam piping.

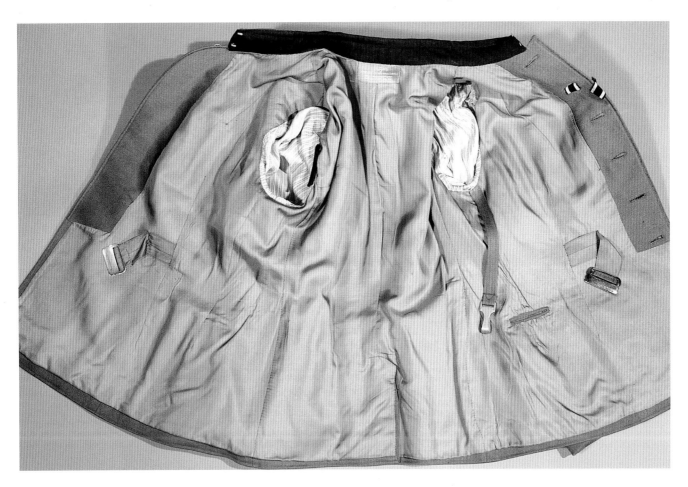

(23) **Artillery officer, service dress, Russia 1943-44**

The development of artillery in the Army had been relatively slow, due to several factors. Firstly, the terms of the Treaty of Versailles did not allow Germany to posses heavy guns in the period between the wars. This was a contributory factor to the adoption of the *"Blitzkreig"* ("lightning war") concept, in which the need for conventional artillery bombardment to prepare the way for assaults was partly offset by the use of direct air support immediately ahead of fast-moving tank and motorised formations. As the war dragged on new types of weapons were developed, out of necessity, in imitation of enemy innovations, or as cost-effective substitutes for more conventional ordnance. The Artillery arm became responsible for a wide range of weapons from field howitzers and garrison guns to anti-aircraft guns used in the anti-tank role (the deadly 8.8cm gun of the *Flakartillerie*), rocket weapons (e.g. the multi-tube rocket-propelled mortar misleadingly termed *Nebelwerfer* or "smoke projector"), self-propelled artillery mounted on tank chassis (*Panzerartillerie*), and even enormous railway guns.

Although the war in the East had by now reduced the appearance of the German soldier to a fairly shabby level, some vestiges of former smartness still remained. Officers still retained the bullion insignia, and while some made use of enlisted ranks' general issue uniforms, many persisted in having these upgraded to an officer's cut.

This tunic started life as an enlisted man's issue M35 pattern; it has been converted for officer's wear as well as being up-dated or repaired at a later date. It retains the four pleated pockets with slightly rounded scalloped flaps, and the five front buttons, of the M35 pattern. The collar, originally covered with dark green badge cloth, has been re-cut to give sharper points and then re-faced. The sleeves have had the cuff vents removed and officer's French cuffs added; and in keeping with fashion the skirt has been shortened. It is interesting to note that the skirt pockets have been replaced during the war; the cloth used is a good but not a perfect match, and machine stitching with different coloured threads shows that the work was not carried out at the time of the original tailor modification.

The lining resembles that of the M35 tunic, but with several alterations, presumably made when the back of the tunic was taken in to fit the wearer. In addition a grey cotton internal pocket has been added at the left breast, as well as a vent behind the left skirt pocket for the hanger of the dress dagger; at some point there was also a cloth suspender extending from the left armpit, but this has been removed. The right panel bears size markings and "H 39" (Hannover 1939) and a hand-written "ART 70" (70.Artillerie-Regiment?).

The insignia include "subdued" silver cord shoulder straps for *Hauptmann* (Captain) and officer's *Litzen*, both with red *Waffenfarbe*, and a hand-embroidered officer's grade breast eagle. The awards consist of the Iron Cross 1st Class, the Army Flak Badge (*Heeres-Flakabzeichen*), a three-place ribbon bar (Iron Cross 2nd Class, War Merit Cross 2nd Class with Swords, and Eastern Winter Campaign 1941/42 medal); and, on the left sleeve, the Demjansk Shield, awarded in April 1943 to personnel participating in the 14-month defence of the "Demjansk Pocket" south of Lake Ilmen in 1941-42.

The breeches are the type issued to mounted personnel,

which were often worn by senior non-commissioned staff and officers. They have three slash pockets secured by buttons, with a small fob pocket at the right groin, and the cuffs are closed with three buttons. There is a waist adjustment tab at the rear, and buttons are provided for braces. The usual reinforcement patch is present, in this case with an unusual "quilting" pattern stitched into the inside knee and calf area. The waistband is marked with the size and "M 41" (Munich 1941).

The M38 "new style" field cap for officers is tailored in a low quality field grade material, typical of the later war years. It follows the basic design of the regulation sidecap, but lacks the ventilation eyelets, and also has a smaller crown, which was deemed to give a better "sit". The silver woven piping denoting officer status is applied around the edges of the crown and at the front scallop. The eagle is machined in silver thread on a field-grey backing; the cockade is worked as a raised boss over a padded former. The interior is lined with a sea-blue cotton and has a leather partial sweatband inside the forehead area only; this band is impressed "Deutsches Qualität" ("German quality").

Above left
A "field grade" example of the standard officer's M38 field cap with Artillery braid soutache; note the unimpressive quality of the material. The eagle is the flat machine-woven pattern while the cockade is worked as a raised boss in heavy bullion (despite a matching machine-woven cockade being available).

Above
The Artillery shoulder straps display the two gilt-finished rank stars of Hauptmann (Captain); and a good example of the "subdued", oxydised silver finish of most wartime-made strap braid. Note the varying shades of the red Waffenfarbe seen here, which is quite common. The hand-embroidered breast eagle is sewn on by hand - a common period practice.

Left
The pattern of the M35 enlisted ranks' tunic is apparent here, with the pleated and scalloped pockets and five-button closure - as are the modification of the cuffs for an officer's wear, and the slighty mismatched appearance of the two skirt pockets due to replacement.

Below
The Iron Cross was always worn higher than any other awards except the Close Combat Clasp. Those on the pocket are attached with the use of sewn loops. The field-grey backing to the Demjansk Shield is sandwiched between the shield itself and a metal backing plate, and sewn to the sleeve.

Bottom
The tunic lining is in a discoloured cream drill

material. On close inspection, the seams from the alterations can be observed around the lower pockets and at either side of the rear panel. Note the grey extra pocket, and the dagger hanger vent.

Right
The size markings and manufacture codes are easy to read on the tunic, but faint on the breeches. Note hand-written "ART 70" on the tunic.

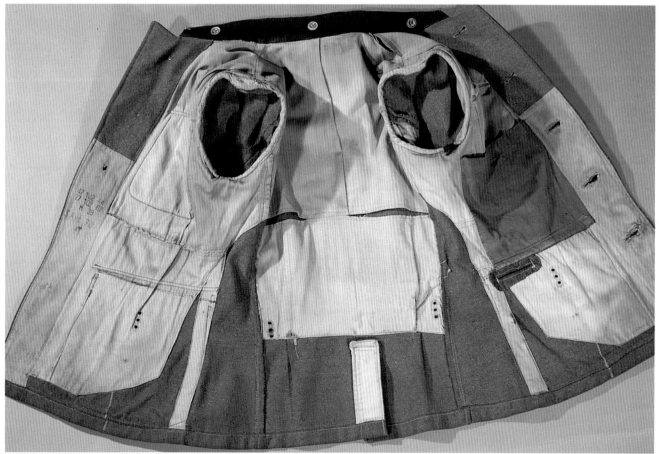

(24) Infantry enlisted man, combat dress, France 1944

When the Allied forces landed in Normandy on 6 June 1944 significant numbers of veteran combat units were in France for rest and reorganisation after extensive experience on the Eastern Front; and within days of the Allied landings the *Wehrmacht* was demonstrating its extraordinary resilience. In the campaign for France the Allies enjoyed complete air superiority, and the German Army found its every daylight movement hounded from the air. Most ground combat in Normandy took place at short ranges in heavy cover. Both factors made the camouflaging of vehicles and men alike an important consderation.

By this time the Army, which had been much slower than the *Waffen-SS* to introduce camouflage clothing, had several garments in regular service. A pullover combat smock (*Tarnhemd*) and a helmet cover in *Splittermuster* pattern reversing to white, which superficially resembled the SS equivalent items, had been issued since 1942, and a later model hooded smock in *Sumpfmuster* appeared in 1943; but these were far from universal issue, and the reversible winter uniform remained the most widely used Army camouflage garment. Some crude body aprons in *Sumpfmuster* pattern were observed; however, the most readily available camouflage garment for most Army troops in summer 1944 remained the shelter section/poncho (*Zeltbahn 31*) issued to all field troops, which was frequently pressed into service as a fast, effective means of personal camouflage.

The *Zeltbahn* was made from high density, water-repellent cotton material cut in the shape of an isosceles triangle, the base measuring 2.5m and the sides about 1.9 metres. By means of corner grommets, 62 steel washer-type buttons and 30 buttonholes, various configurations could be made up. Its main purpose was as a bivouac tent: by buttoning two, three, or more together, and using the issue tent poles, a small weather-proof tent was constructed. A central flapped vent also allowed it to be worn over the head as a poncho; once again, through the use of various buttoning patterns it could be configured for wear on horseback, while riding a bicycle, or on foot. The *Zeltbahn* was printed with the Army's *Splittermuster* camouflage, one side in lighter, the other in darker shades; it was not made in the later *Sumpfmuster* ("tan water") camouflage. The *Zeltbahn* was initially stamped and dated by the manufacturer near to one of the corners, but this is usually no longer discernible; later examples sometimes show an *RB-Nummer* only.

The factory-made camouflage helmet cover (*Tarnhelmuberzug*) was not very widely used, although "field expedient" covers were common. The issue cover was made in "splinter" camouflage reversing to white, and was sewn from five panels; a second model featured seven loops sewn around the outside for the attachment of foliage. The cover was secured by a drawstring around the edge, unlike the more complex *Waffen-SS* system of sprung hooks. Many field-manufactured covers may be encountered which are cut from *Zeltbahn* material, and therefore have "splinter" camouflage printed on both sides. Field-made covers in *Sumpfmuster* pattern, made by cutting up late-model smocks or winter uniforms, are much rarer.

This soldier wears the battle pack (*Gefechtsgepäck*) attached to the rear of his combat braces. This heavy webbing A-frame provided a means for carrying the basic requirements for combat where the full knapsack would be cumbersome. At each of the four tips D-rings with hooks could be engaged to the combat braces and their auxiliary straps. Two stowage straps attached to the lower part of the frame could be buckled round the rolled *Zeltbahn*; the messtin was attached above this by slipping its retaining strap through slots in the web frame. A canvas bag was also issued with the pack, to hold items from the breadbag such as the rifle cleaning kit, field stove, eating utensils, iron rations, etc., but this was often omitted in practice.

The entrenching tool (*kleines Schanzzeug*) was carried by most combat troops. The most common variety was the "square" pattern seen here; there was a later folding pattern (*Klappspaten*) with a pointed blade which could be locked in three positions for carrying, digging, and use as a pick. These tools were slung from the belt in leather carrier frames, with the bayonet scabbard secured - to keep it steady - against the tool haft by the carrier fastening strap. This assistant gunner of an MG42 machine gun crew carries two 300-round ammunition tins (*Patronenkasten 41*), as well as a spare barrel carrier (*Laufschüter 42*).

Above left
The second pattern issue helmet cover with foliage loops. Note that while other field-made covers are encountered, this is the only official issue type; it will normally be found printed in Splittermuster camouflage on one side, reversing to natural unbleached off-white.

Above
The "small entrenching tool" was almost unchanged since the 1880s; it was sometimes sharpened for use as a hand-to-hand weapon. The S84/98 bayonet remained unchanged during the war except for the substitution of bakelite for wooden grips; the frog has the hilt retaining strap added during the war.

Left
The 1931 pattern Zeltbahn. Note the triangular shape; the placing of the buttons, buttonholes and grommets; the central vent for the head when worn as a poncho, with cover flaps; and the differing shades on the two sides. While the basic pattern is constant, colour variations will be found due to dispersed manufacture.

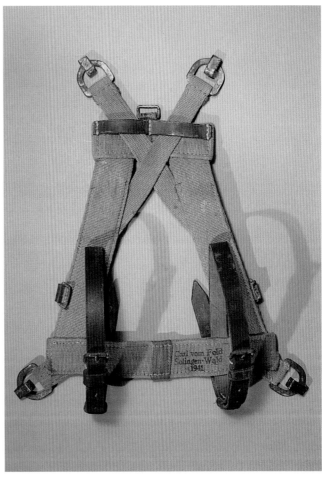

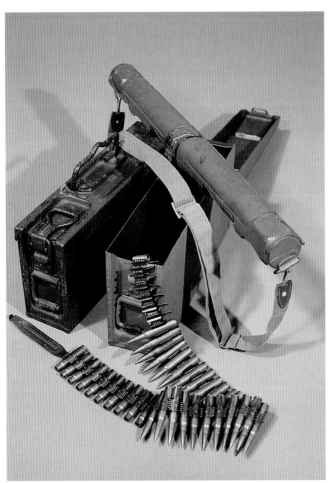

Above left
The battle pack, inside surface, showing the structure and durable materials, and the four hooks in the corners for attachment to the braces.

Above right
The battle pack from the rear, showing the attached straps for the Zeltbahn or bedroll; note also the manufacturer's stamp for "Carl Vom Feld Solingen-Wald 1941".

Left
The ammunition cans held 300 rounds or one 250-round non-disintegrating link belt; note the off-set handle to make it easier to carry two tins, or to sling them over the shoulder at each end of a strap. This model of spare barrel canister held one barrel for either the MG34 or MG42.

(25) Armoured Infantry enlisted man, greatcoat combat dress, Russia 1943-44

By 1944 the German textile industry had reached a critical point in the production of fabric for the manufacture of uniforms. Since 1942 an increasing proportion of rayon had been substituted for wool on economic grounds. However, by this date industry was also reduced to pulping scrap material and reconstituting it into bolts of field-grey fabric. These shoddy materials, which were used in most late war clothing, had poor insulation qualities, tore more easily than wool, and retained moisture, being harder to dry when wet. By the 1944-45 period the wool content of most uniforms was below 30%, and the cotton liner material of earlier days had been replaced by a grey spun rayon. Leather for field equipment was also in short supply; an *Ersatz* alternative was found by applying a lacquer made from timber pulp over layers of thin web sheet or pressed cardboard. This so-called *Press-Stoff*, made in both black and tan finishes, was used to produce items such as pistol holsters, pouches and entrenching tool carriers. Thus, while the outline of the soldier appeared basically unchanged, the quality and durability of his uniform and equipment had suffered markedly from Germany's ever-worsening economic position.

The greatcoat had undergone several changes since the start of the war, mainly for economic reasons. The coat was still double-breasted and closed with two rows of six front buttons, with a single resin button securing the right front panel to the lining of the left panel. The length of the coat was to about mid-calf, and the sleeves were still finished with a French cuff. Two slash pockets with slanted flaps were provided at hip level, and a single pocket inside the left breast lining. The collar, its dark green badge cloth facing replaced by field-grey since 1940, had altered in size. The original collars were 9cm deep at the front, but by the end of the war some were almost double this size. The example shown is the most regularly encountered, being of roughly median size. The underside of the collar was fitted with a tab with two buttonholes, allowing it to be turned up and buttoned across the lower face; there was also a hook and eye at the throat to close the base of the collar when worn normally.

The rear of the coat had an integral half-belt with two standard buttons and buttonholes which theoretically allowed adjustment of the waist; it was rarely used. There was an open pleat running down from the back of the neck to the waist (which remains sewn closed on this illustrated example, contrary to regulations); below the half-belt the skirt was vented, the vent being closed at need by four small resin buttons. The shoulders were fitted with a cloth bridle and buttons for slip-on shoulder straps; those seen here are for a *Panzergrenadier*, an enlisted man of the (nominally) armoured half-track infantry units integral to the Armoured and Armoured Infantry Divisions. The lining is cut from a light drab drill material and covers the inside from the waist up, with two hanging pockets; the sleeves are lined with a single layer of silver-grey artificial cotton. Above the pockets at each hip is a vertical opening which allowed the belt hooks on the tunic to reach through and support the belt order worn over the greatcoat. This coat has a size marking only, stamped on the internal left breast pocket, although additional markings may be found inside.

This section machine gunner is wearing the standard belt order for his duties. On the issue belt, at the left hip, he wears a softshell holster for the Walther P38 pistol; all machine gunners were issued sidearms for personal protection. The holster is made of smooth leather (pebbled finishes will be encountered) with vertical and horizontal flaps; on the front is a holder for a spare magazine. The rear has two belt loops and extensive markings: between the loops is the manufacturer's code "bla 1944" (for E.G.Leuner, Bautzen) and the *Waffenampt* proof stamp below this; to the right of the loops is a large stamped outline "P38". Another standard piece of equipment was the gunner's spares pouch (*Werkzeugtasche*) worn at the right of the belt. This contained essential accessories such as spare bolt and firing pin assemblies, anti-aircraft sight, tools, oil, cleaning gear, and muzzle cover; an asbetos pad for handling hot barrels was often carried under the front fastening strap. While the spares pouch is found in leather, this example is made from *Press-Stoff*; the front strap is leather, as are the two belt loops at the rear. An iron D-ring was also attached to allow fitting of the combat braces.

Below
The M42 helmet with its distinctive uncrimped rim. This example has what appears to be a factory applied slate-grey paint finish with a rough texture. No transfer insignia were applied by this date.

Right
This is the most commonly encountered pattern of late-war greatcoat, made of degraded quality cloth with a low wool content, and with a medium depth field-grey collar.

Bottom
The standard coat lining extends only from the waist up. Note the hanging hip pockets, the silver-grey sleeve lining, the vents for the belt support hooks, and the buttons to close the skirt vent.

Opposite top
This type of collar closure tab is found on almost all greatcoats and protective coats.

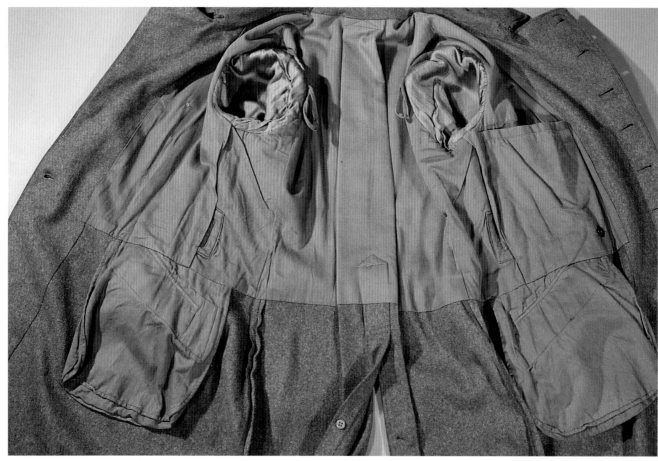

Left
Many machine gun crews carried binoculars (Doppelfernröhre) for spotting targets. These are the standard issue 6x30 type, with a manufacturer's code "cag" (for D.Swarovski Glasfabrik, Wattens/Tyrol).

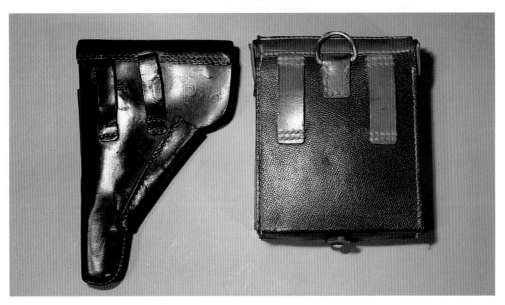

Left
The rear of the semi-automatic pistol holster displays the manufacture markings (see main text) between the belt loops and "P38" to the right. The rear of the machine gunner's spares pouch shows its composite construction, with leather belt loops, suspender ring strap and fastening strap sewn to textured synthetic "Press-Stoff".

(26) Armoured Troops NCO, vehicle combat dress, France 1944

The importance of the Armoured branch remained undiminished throughout the war. Despite heavy losses, the introduction of formidable new tanks such as the PzKw V Panther and PzKw VI Tiger, and the enormous accumulated battle experience of young unit commanders, kept the employment of armour at the heart of German counter-offensive and defensive tactics on all fronts. German armour repeatedly tipped the balance of both minor and major engagements; the losses inflicted on Russian armour were incredibly high, proving time and again that quality and experience could outweigh greatly superior numbers. When the Allies landed in France in June 1944 they brought with them a vast array of new armoured vehicles manned by diligent and enthusiastic crews; but the minority of North African veterans among them also brought a deep respect for the enemy and his equipment. Once again, relatively small numbers of technically superior tanks crewed by Russian Front veterans would exact a high price for every mile the Allies advanced.

The black vehicle uniform was, by this time, worn by various specialist troops other than tank crews, including Armoured Signals, Engineers, Reconnaissance, and even some units of Armoured Artillery. For tank units the vehicle service and combat dress remained largely unchanged during the course of the war. The most noticeable simplification was the omission of the *Waffenfarbe* piping around the collar from some time in 1942. The jacket illustrated, while being one of a limited number manufactured as early as 1940 without the collar piping, illustrates the uniform which was predominantly seen in the latter half of the war.

The jacket remains the short, double-breasted pattern without external pockets, the front being fastened at the right waist with four large resin buttons hidden behind a fly. The left lapel also has three buttonholes to engage three smaller buttons on the right breast which, together with a hook and eye at the throat, allow the front to be secured across against the elements. The collar retains the more pointed cut of the M36 pattern; and the plain cuff has the regular adjustable rear vent. The lining, which remained unchanged in cut, is made here of the earlier light grey drill fabric; this was replaced in later jackets by artificial satin in silver-grey or black. Only the front panels are lined, from the base to the shoulder. Two internal patch pockets are provided, that on the right having a horizontal opening and that on the left a vertical opening. On either side of the rear waist is a small "tunnel" containing a double tape for adjusting the fit. A tab for a belt support hook hangs down from each armpit, with the hooks protruding through one of four horizontal slits. The lining is stamped above the left pocket with the sizes and "Paul Opalla & Co. B40" (Berlin 1940).

The insignia consist of the universal rhomboid-shaped collar patches with white metal death's-heads and *Waffenfarbe* piping; an early pattern breast eagle machine-woven in white on black; and shoulder straps displaying the rank of *Unterfeldwebel* (Sergeant) by a complete border of matt silver *Tresse* braid. As already mentioned in section 21, NCO *Tresse* was never applied around the collar of the vehicle uniform. This tank commander wears the ribbons for the War Merit Cross 2nd Class and the Eastern Winter Campaign 1941/42 medal in his lapel, and has the Tank Battle Badge (*Panzer-*

kampfabzeichen) pinned to the left breast - this was awarded for participation in three different tank assaults.

Soft attached-collar shirts, initially in mouse-grey and later in field-grey, were worn with a black tie. The trousers for the vehicle uniform remained unchanged, apart from the occasional replacement of the internal belt with belt loops. The field cap is of the standard M34 pattern, as introduced in black for Armoured Troops during March 1940. The form of the insignia is conventional, but with the national eagle machine-woven in white (later, grey) on black, above a national cockade on black. The soutache in rose-pink *Waffenfarbe* was abolished in July 1942, but in practice continued to be seen until the war's end. The M42 and M43 field caps were also issued in black, but the M34 pattern was the most popular as it did not interfere with the use of headphones and optics.

The headphones are the *Funkhaube A* pattern for use by armoured vehicle crews, with large hollow rubber pads round the earpieces for comfort and to keep out noise. The throat microphone (*Kehlkopfmikrofon*) is the type used by tank crews, with a small junction box hanging on the chest with a lockable push-to-talk button.

above left & above
The M34 field cap, introduced in black cloth during 1940 and identical in construction to the field-grey version. Caps were lined with either grey or black cotton twill. Markings can include the manufacturer's details and size, or simply the size; this example is stamped "Franze Ritter vorn Karl Roth Dettingen 1942" and sized "58".

Left
An interesting example of the black Panzer jacket which follows the post-1942 pattern (without collar piping), despite being marked as manufactured in 1940. Note the arrangement of buttons and buttonholes, and compare with the privately tailored version in section 8.

Right
The collar patches and breast eagle remain standard; this early white-on-black breast eagle was replaced by a light grey pattern on jackets manufactured from the mid-war years. The shoulder straps for Unterfeldwebel are the early sewn-in type; later patterns were detachable - although they are very occasionally encountered sewn down to the shoulder all round to avoid snagging inside the tank.

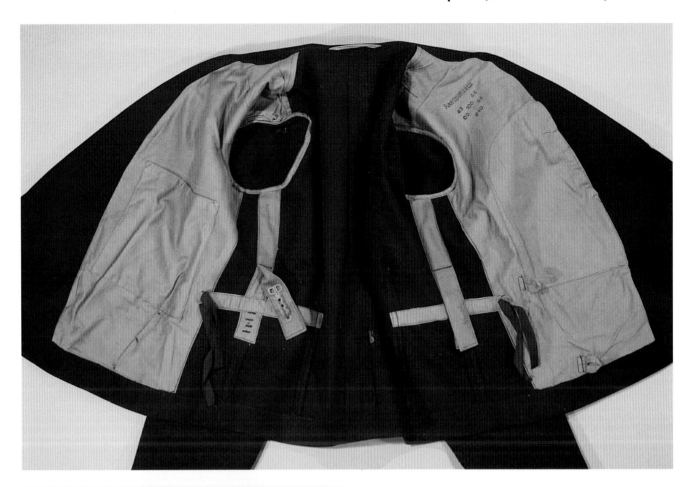

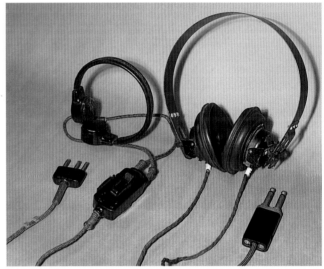

Top
The standard pattern of lining for the Panzer jacket, which remained unchanged during the war apart from materials. Note the belt support hook in its hanging tab, the pockets, and the adjustment laces.

Above
These headphones are a late manufacture example of the Funkhaube A, lacking the usual leather or leatherette sleeve covering the sprung metal headband; note the rubber earpads. The throat microphones are illustrated complete with the small junction box with the push-to-talk button on the front.

(27) Infantry officer, M44 service dress, Germany 1944-45

In the summer of 1943 field tests were conducted on a new type of service uniform which was intended for use by all field units of the armed services. The design, a marked departure from any of the existing patterns, was intended to save in both raw materials and manufacturing costs. The result was the 1944 pattern field service dress, which represented the last stage in the wartime evolution of the German uniform. The traditional four-pocket tunic gave place to a two-pocket, waist-length blouse which superficially resembled the British 1937 battledress blouse. Because of the high proportion of synthetic fibres used in the material the dye colour was altered; the official designation was Field-Grey M44 (*Feldgrau M44*), which was an olive shade with a slight brownish cast to it; but many shades of grey and green will also be encountered. The new *Feldbluse M44* proved unpopular with some, who mourned the departure from the traditional German tunic design - and noted the practical disadvantage that the short jacket tended to ride up, pulling away from the trousers. Others welcomed it, however, for its simplicity and for the neat appearance which could sometimes be achieved.

The M44 field blouse was a waist-length jacket closed with six front buttons, the bottom two being placed on a deep waistband. There were two unpleated patch pockets on the chest, with straight-cut buttoned flaps. The sleeves had simplified cuff vents, the adjustment buttonholes for the resin buttons being placed in the sleeve itself rather than being concealed on a tape sewn to the inside of the vent. The collar was cut slightly longer and more pointed than that of the previous tunic, and while it could be buttoned to the top there was no hook and eye at the throat; the collar was rarely worn closed, but open with the upper lapels folded flat. The M44 blouse was lined, inside the two front panels only, usually with a dull grey rayon material; various other shades will also be encountered. The field dressing pocket was deleted, but the blouse had an internal pocket in each breast, closed by single buttons. A belt hook support tab extended from below each armpit, with only one vent in each side of the waistband for passing the hook through.

There was no distinct officer's version of this blouse. However, as officers were entitled to draw them from unit stores, it was not unusual for them to have the officer's grade insignia substituted. The fact that some officers found this blouse quite attractive is indicated by the existence of a number of privately tailored copies. This *Oberleutnant* has the slip-on field grade shoulder straps for his rank with white *Waffenfarbe* for Infantry. The standard field grade collar *Litzen* are worn, once again with white *Waffenfarbe*. A new version of these patches appeared from September 1944, machine-woven in one piece with affixed *Waffenfarbe* strips; but these were rarely seen, and never replaced the silver hand-embroidered type to any significant extent. The breast eagle is the conventional hand-made pattern in silver. By this date there was also a flat machine-woven version worked on a dark green triangular backing, which did see limited use. This officer displays the *Infanterie-Sturmabzeichen*, and a ribbon bar for the Iron Cross 2nd Class and the Eastern Winter Campaign 1941/42 medal.

The breeches (*Stiefelhose*) are a privately tailored pair, of

"field" as opposed to "dress" quality; the material is a coarse, late war grey wool. To many officers the breeches and riding boots were a mark of their commissioned status and were carefully retained. The officer's version of the *Einheitsfeldmütze 43* is seen here; basically of the same design as the enlisted ranks' version, it is distinguished by silver-coloured piping around the crown seam (this was gold for general officer ranks). The machine-woven insignia, worked on a single truncated triangular field-grey backing like the enlisted ranks' pattern, featured a silver eagle and silver ring in the cockade. While this flat-woven badge is regulation and the type most commonly seen, there are many examples of private modifications such as the wearing of hand-embroidered bullion insignia, and extra piping at the front scallop.

This officer is wearing the riding boots, the officer's service belt, and a black holster for the Walther P38 pistol. He is arming a *Tellermine 43*, which was one of a series of anti-tank "plate" mines.

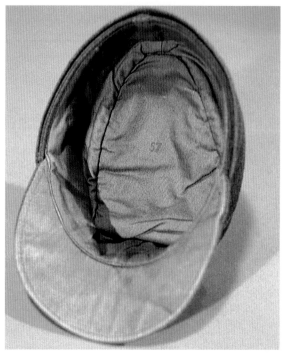

Above left & above
The officer's version of the Einheitsfeldmütze M43 proved to be very popular; there is plentiful photographic evidence for its use even by general officers. Note that this late manufacture cap has the ventilation eyelets omitted. It may possibly be a privately purchased example, as it displays the unusual feature of the lining cloth extended to cover the underside of the peak. Note that the only marking is for size.

Left
While its popularity and use among officers were far from universal, the M44 field blouse could look tolerably smart in a no-nonsense, front line style if fully badged. Most officers preferred to retain the four-pocket service tunic, however. The open collar of the blouse required a collar-attached shirt to be worn; at this date it was common for officers to use the field-grey general issue item.

Left
The insignia, for an
Oberleutnant of Infantry,
remind us that the hand-
embroidered officer's
insignia were used right up
to the end of the war,
despite the introduction of
some machine-woven
equivalents.

Above
The 1943 model Tellermine
was one of four commonly
used anti-tank mines; it had
a mushroom-shaped
pressure plate and contained
12 pounds of TNT. Note the
stencilled markings.

Top
This interior view of the
blouse shows the two
internal pockets and the belt
hook tabs. Just visible high
inside the right breast is the
outline of the removed and
replaced factory-applied
breast eagle.

(28) Armoured Infantry enlisted man, M44 combat dress, Germany 1945

In spring 1945 the *Wehrmacht* had their backs to the wall, fighting the Anglo-American armies advancing from the west and from Italy, and the Red Army flooding into Germany from the east. As the *Reich* was overrun and dismembered the military situation descended into chaos; the remnants of some units fought heroic last-ditch actions, while others disintegrated amid a mood of "every man for himself". Veteran soldiers, hastily conscripted boys and elderly home guards fought together under purely local command, striving simply to survive - and, wherever possible, to surrender to the Western Allies rather than the more vengeful Russians. The infrastructure of command and control, supply and support had largely broken down, and the troops had to make do with whatever they could find. The issue of the M44 uniform had been on a priority basis, with fighting units such as *Panzergrenadiers* being first in line, but it was available in numbers too small to change the overall appearance of the German Army. Those who did receive it, however, demonstrated the transformation which had taken place between the invasion of Poland on 1 September 1939 and the surrender of Germany on 7 May 1945. The fine quality, impressively adorned uniform of the German soldier, clearly recalling the Prussian traditions of the 19th century, had become a drab, shapeless outfit more befitting a labourer or mechanic, constructed from the shoddiest *Ersatz* materials.

The M44 blouse illustrated was part of a bundle looted from a clothing factory near Hannover in 1945, and appears exactly as it did when awaiting issue. The finish in this case is still of a respectable quality, although the materials would probably not withstand a great deal of punishment; the cloth still exhibits the field-grey colour of earlier tunics. The M44 uniform will be encountered in basically three different fabrics. The first is the regular field-grey material seen here, which had been used for earlier uniforms. The second type is referred to as "*Russischer-Stoff*" or "Russian material": this is field-grey with a slightly brownish cast, reportedly because of the use of pulped Russian uniform fabric mixed in during the manufacture of substitute (*Ersatz*) cloth. The third type of fabric encountered is a dull grey material which was taken from stocks in Italy: several M44 Army and *Waffen-SS* uniforms have been encountered in this cloth. The tunic lining is made of a "bronze-silver" rayon material, with a buttoned patch pocket inside each breast. Stampings are limited to size measurements, and these appear above the left inside pocket.

While the tunic is made from the first type field-grey material, the shoulder straps - original to this jacket since 1945 - are manufactured from "*Russischer-Stoff*". They are of the late war pattern, with no backing other than a reinforcing strip of rayon under the strap and tongue. The collar patches are the standard wartime *Litzen* introduced after 1940. The breast eagle is the last pattern used, with the backing patch sewn on as a triangle (instead of being cut and folded to the outline of the eagle) to save manufacturing time. A late war screen-printed version also exists, though it is quite rare.

The regulation M44 service trousers are seen here in the third type or "Italian" material. They have two front and two rear pockets and a fob pocket, all with straight flaps closed with a single button. There are external belt loops, but a web belt with buckle is included. Some trousers had this belt sewn on internally, with a two-claw buckle; others, as here, had the belt attached externally, with a three-claw buckle. The legs were cut straight, with an internal drawstring or button tab at the ankle to allow gathering under the gaiters. All buttons were of the resin type, with buttons for braces still provided. The ankle boots and gaiters are worn here.

The standard M43 field cap is worn, and has changed little since its introduction. While the early linings were in a grey cotton, grey "herringbone" weave rayon was used in late manufacture examples. Markings were usually limited to a size or the "RB" number. Application of the metal ventilation eyelets was also stopped.

As a prisoner of war (*Kriegsgefangener*) this soldier has been allowed to retain his basic subsistence equipment for use in the camps. Being a young recruit his gear is almost new: the service buckle in the late dark grey colour on a thin *Ersatz* leather belt, the breadbag, and the attached waterbottle and messtin. He is offering his *Soldbuch* for inspection.

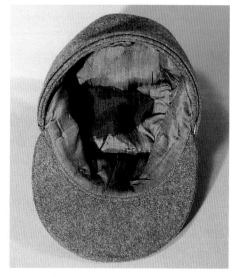

Above left & above
Late manufacture M43 field cap. The buttons are now painted in the same dark grey as used on the belt buckle; and note the absence of ventilation eyelets. The later caps used a lining in grey "herringbone" rayon. The dark patch is a period stain; this cap carries no markings whatever.

Left
The M44 Feldbluse, the last pattern of enlisted ranks' jacket issued before the end of the war. The general similarity to the British 1937 battledress blouse and the US Army's olive drab wool field jacket ("Ike jacket") is obvious. This example, complete with its insignia, is exactly as it was found unissued in a German factory in 1945.

Right
The late model shoulder straps, backed only by a strip of rayon along the strap and the retaining tongue, are made of a cloth distinctly different from the blouse; this is the so-called "Russian material", in grey of a faintly brownish cast. The collar patches are the standard mid- to late war type. The breast eagle is now sewn on as a triangle to save labour.

Left
Note the colour of the rayon lining material; the belt support hook in its suspension tab; and the internal breast pockets, with size stampings above the left pocket.

Below
Details of the M44 service trousers, in this case made from the "Italian" type material (which was also used to produce jackets). Note the straight pocket flaps, the attached external belt with three-claw buckle, and the button adjustment tab at the ankle.

(29) Personal Equipment and Effects

(1) Zeltbahn 31 shelter section/poncho in "splinter" camouflage (note contrast between lighter and darker sides in this unfaded, probably unissued example). The piece is marked "B35" (Berlin 1935), and bears the almost illegible stamp of a manufacturer (Anton Jöring ?)

(2) Kochgeschirr 31, the soldier's 1.7 litre "cookpot" or messtin set, this example in olive-painted aluminium marked "O.H.W.44" on the handle attachment plate of the lid.

(3) Aluminium 0.8 litre Feldflasche 31 waterbottle (this example marked "S.K.N.39" on the neck), in its snap-fastened brown felt insulating cover, with the black-painted aluminium cup (marked "W.A.L.39") which was carried strapped over the screw cap.

(4) M38 gasmask, the olive fabric covering a one-piece light grey rubber facemask; plentifully marked, it has "A Flr 44" embossed on the filter attachment; the screw-on filter is marked "Fe 41". The head straps are canvas.

(5) The M38 canister (Tragbüsche für Gasmaske M38) – distinguishable from the M30 pattern by its shallower lid – has spare eyepieces stowed inside the lid, with (in this example) a hand-written tape "Gefr.Schmeidek Rudolf 2/Bau Ers.Batl.17" (Senior Private Rudolf Schmeidek, 2nd Company, 17th Replacement Construction Battalion).

(6) The gas sheet (Gasplane), intended to protect against sprayed agents, was of treated fabric or paper and is found in many colours; this olive example is of treated paper and is marked "gch", "81/41/3", "80g". Its field-grey oilcloth bag (this one marked "Gebruder Wendler GMBH") is carried looped onto the gasmask canister sling. Lying on the bag here is a brown plastic box marked "ET", "1940", with instruction label headed "Hautentgiftungsmittel" - skin decontamination remedy. These tablets were carried in the gasmask canister.

(7) The small kit stowage bag for the A-frame combat pack (Beutel zum Gefechtsgepäck); the rifle cleaning kit is carried inside the flap.

(8) Black bakelite example of the fat container (Fettbüsche), for lard, butter, etc., carried in the breadbag.

(9) Packet of 50 cigarette papers, Efka Pyramiden brand.

(10) Twenty oval-section cigarettes in beige card wartime economy pack marked "Sondermischung" (special blend) and priced at 4 pfennigs.

(11) Six "Merkur" cigarettes in coloured pack, markings including Bulgarian/Macedonian origin.

(12) Goggles with olive rubber facepiece embossed "Neophon", round red lenses and olive web strap, complete with green fabric pouch; and a pair of goggles with green/yellow lenses in aluminium and wire mesh frames, with black elastic strap.

(13) Model 1911 triple rifle cartridge pouches, stamped on centre rear "RBNr 0/0561/0050".

(30) Personal Equipment and Effects

(1) The Fettbüsche is more usually found in brown or orange bakelite than the black of the previous example.

(2) Cigars were as popular as cigarettes during the war. The band is marked "Für Deutsche Wehrmacht Steuerfrei" ("For the German Armed Forces - tax-free").

(3) This packet of 25 cigarettes is typical of the Russian type which were also available to the troops after 1941. The darker portion is the tobacco; the white area is a cardboard holder.

(4) This "trench lighter" is made from an 8mm cartridge head-stamped 1944. The dummy head comes off to reveal the wick, which is lit by the striker at the side; filling is through the primer hole in the base.

(5) The Esbit field stove was a folding metal tray assembly which held burning solid fuel tablets; the messtin was placed above the open top. The tablets were stored inside when the cooker was folded closed for carrying in the breadbag or the A-frame bag.

(6) The rifle cleaning kit M34 (Reinigungsgeräte M34) for the Mauser Karabiner 98k consisted of a metal tin with brushes, a chain pull-through, an oiler and cleaning tools in one end, and cleaning patches in the other.

(7) Feldpost writing paper was issued for the all-important letters home. Each unit had a Feldpost number.

(8) Through the Feldpost, soldiers occasionally received amusements such as this chess set with cardboard pieces and folding board.

(9) The issue service glasses (Dienstbrille). This unissued pair were made by Rodenstok; once issued they would be carried in a grey metal tin marked "Dienst-Brille".

(10) The service glasses for wear with the gasmask (Masken-Brille) were the same as the regular glasses but with tapes instead of arms at the side so as not to effect the seal of the mask against the face.

(11) Items such as soap and razors were sold by military canteens.

(12) The singing of marching songs was a feature of marching and rest-breaks in the German Army, and was officially encouraged during training; books like this, giving the words of many popular songs, were widely available.

(13) Condoms were made available to the troops either singly or in small packets. A tropical model was also issued.

(14) The Model 1910 folding fork/spoon combination was issued to the troops, and a knife/fork/spoon combination was privately available. This one is marked on the fork "Igk & F 42".

(15) The M31 breadbag (Brotbeutel) was carried on the rear of the belt, and held items such as these for the soldier's everyday use, plus towel, sewing kit, field cap, iron ration, meat container, etc. (though not all at once). The bag will be found in many shades of field-grey, grey, green and brown.

(31) Personal Equipment

(1) These hand-cranked torches were practical because they did not require a battery; a charge was generated by pressing in a plunger. The green torch was made by Phillips in occupied Holland, the other is a Braun Manulux.

(2) These flashlights are two of the more popular types of the many available. Both have a button tab at the top, and two colour filter slides for signalling.

(3) The "Juwel 33" was a heater and stove which ran on vaporised petrol. The canister has a screw-off lid with a folding cooker stand and includes filling and adjustment tools.

(4) The general purpose goggles had a leather mask with an elastic headband and glass lenses. The Eyeshield 42 (Augenschützer 42) was a basically disposable plastic goggle and came in a paper packet. Both came with clear and smoked lenses.

(5) The M35 mapcase came in black or brown leather with a variety of fittings. There were usually three compartments for maps, scales, and notebooks with holders on the front for pencils, rubbers, slide rules, etc. It usually had two belt loops at the back.

(6) Compasses will be found in a variety of styles, that shown being fairly common. It is fitted in a fold-open plastic body with a chrome mirror, and is marked "Marsch Kompass" on the lid.

(7) All soldiers wore the identification tag (Erkennungsmarken) around the neck. It was an oval perforated plate in light metal with the unit title, the owner's roster number and his blood group stamped on each half. If the owner was killed the plate was snapped along the perforation, the upper half remaining on the body while the other was returned for records.

(8) First aid dressings were issued to all troops and carried in a special pocket in the field uniform. The style of the packaging changed over time. The green example is marked 1940, the grey packet 1943, and the beige dressing is a special type for the left hand.

(9) A trench knife was often carried, both as a weapon and a general utility knife. Variants existed but the basic style was the same, with wooden grips and a short blued scabbard. Some have a spring clip on the back while others have a leather retainer and belt loop, as here.

(10) Tent pegs were issued for use with the Zeltbahn. The early issue type were in steel, later wartime examples in red-brown bakelite or plastic-impregnated wood.

(11) Tent poles were also issued with the Zeltbahn, made of wood with an iron socket at the top and a guide band near the base. A number of these were joined to achieve the desired height.

(32) Personal Documents

(1) The Soldbuch (soldier's paybook) was issued to all members of the armed forces. It recorded all particulars of the soldier including: issue of kit, units served, medical records, weapons issue, leave taken, pay records, etc. The owner's photograph (usually in uniform) was attached to the inside cover. A small compartment inside the back cover was provided for additional papers. The book shown is for a Karl Berger, who was a Pioneer in a railway maintenance unit. Also shown are his personal data sheet recorded by the British upon his capture; and the cover of a Soldbuch.

(2) The Wehrpass was issued to all personnel when they registered for conscription. It served as a personal identification and recorded all pre-military service (such as RAD). After induction into the armed forces the book was replaced by the Soldbuch and maintained with the soldier's unit records, any relevant information being entered. The example shown is for a Gefreiter Franz Josef Prichoda, who was killed in action on the Russian Front on 14 August 1943 while serving with a unit of the 4th Panzer Army. Also shown is his award document for a posthumous Iron Cross 2nd Class, along with the medal; and a private purchase wallet that held his documents.

(3) The military driver's licence was printed on oilcloth and carried with the Soldbuch. It bore the owner's photograph and details of the types of vehicle he was qualified to operate. This example is for Unteroffizier Walter Jifland of 2nd Company, 27th Signals Battalion (Nachrichten Abteilung 27), and authorises him to drive a motor vehicle (Verbrennungsmaschine).

(4) Medical personnel who wore the Red Cross armband were issued an oilcloth identification document (Personalausweis) which authorised them to do so, conferring the appropriate protection under the Geneva Convention. The document shown is for Gefreiter Heinrich Rott; it lists his date and place of birth, and his position of stretcher bearer (Krankenträger). Below this the document quotes the relevant article of the Convention.

(5) Most combat awards came with an award document which was usually kept in the rear compartment of the Soldbuch. This example follows the usual format, and records the award of the Infantry Assault Badge (Infanterie-Sturmabzeichen) in Silver to Unteroffizier Johann Meyer of 14th Company, 146th Grenadier Regiment (14./Gren.Rgt.146). Also shown is the badge itself.

General glossary, German/English:

Abzeichen	Badge		Kraftradfahrer	Motorcycle rider
Adler	Eagle		Kragen	Collar
Alterer Art	Old style or pattern		Kragenspiegel	Collar patch
Arbeitsanzug	Fatigue dress		Krieg	War
Artillerie	Artillery		Leuchtpistole	Flare pistol
Aufklärung	Reconnaissance		Litzen	Braid (collar)
Ausgehanzug	Walking-out dress		Mantel	Greatcoat
Ausrüstung	Equipment		Marschstiefel	Marching boot
Befehlshaber	Senior commander		Maschinengewehr	Machine gun
Bergmütze	Mountain cap		Maschinenpistole	Sub-machine gun
Blitz	Lightning		Mütze	Cap
Brotbeutel	Breadbag		Nachrichtentruppen	Signals troops
Dienstanzug	Service dress		Nebeltruppen	Smoke troops
Dienstgrade	Rank		Neuer Art	New style
Dienstrock	Service tunic		Oberkommando des Heers	Army High Command
Dolch	Dagger		Oberkommando der Wehrmacht	Armed Forces High Command
Doppelfernröhre	Binoculars		Offizier	Officer
Ehrenzeichen	Decoration		Panzer	Tank, armour
Einheitsfeldmütze	Standard field cap		Panzerabwehr	Anti-tank
Eiserne Kreuz	Iron Cross		Panzergrenadiere	Mechanised infantry
Ersatz	Replacement		Panzerjäger	Tank destroyer
Fabrik	Factory, manufacturer		Panzertruppen	Armoured (tank) troops
Fahne	Flag		Paradeanzug	Parade dress
Feld	Field		Pionier	Engineer
Feldanzug	Field dress		Pistole	Pistol
Feldausrüstung	Field equipment		Rangabzeichen	Badge of rank
Feldbluse	Field blouse		Reiter	Cavalryman
Feldflasche	Waterbottle		Ringkragen	Gorget
Feldgrau	Field-grey		Ritterkreuz	Knight's Cross of the Iron Cross
Feldhose	Field trousers		Rock	Jacket
Feldmütze	Field cap		Säbel	Sabre
Feldstiefel	Field boots		Schirmmütze	Peaked service cap
Führer	Leader		Schulterstücke	Shoulder strap
Funker	Radio operator		Schützenabzeichen	Marksmanship lanyard
Gamaschen	Gaiters		Schwert	Sword
Gasmaske	Gas mask		Soldat	Soldier
Gebirgstruppen	Mountain troops		Soldbuch	Paybook
Gefangener	Prisoner		Spaten	Spade
Gummistoff	Rubberised fabric		Stahlhelm	Steel helmet
Hakenkreuz	Swastika		Stiefelhose	Riding breeches
Handbekleidung	Gloves		Sturmgeschütz	Assault gun
Heer	Army		Tarnanzug	Camouflage dress
Hoheitszeichen	National emblem		Totenkopf	Death's-head
Hose	Trousers		Tornister	Pack, knapsack
Infanterie	Infantry		Tresse	Rank braid (for NCOs)
Jäger	Rifleman		Truppenkennzeichen	Unit shoulder strap cipher
Kavallerie	Cavalry		Vortsösse	Piping
Knöpfe	Button		Wachanzug	Guard dress
Kokarde	Cockade		Waffenfarbe	Branch of service colour
Kommandant	Commander		Waffenrock	Uniform jacket
Koppel	Belt		Wehrmacht	Armed forces
Koppelschloss	Belt buckle		Weisser Rock	White tunic
Koppeltraggestell	Belt support braces		Windjacke	Windjacket
Kraftfahrer	Vehicle driver		Zeltbahn	Shelter section

Select Bibliography

Ailsby, Christopher, *Combat Medals of the Third Reich*, Patrick Stephens Ltd., Northamptonshire, UK (1987)

Angolia, John R. & Schlicht, Adolph, *Uniforms and Traditions of the German Army*, 3 vols., R.James Bender Publishing Co., San Jose CA, USA (1984)

Argyle, Christopher, *Chronology of World War II*, Marshall Cavendish Books Ltd., London, UK (1980)

Baer, Ludwig, *The History of the German Steel Helmet from 1916 to 1945*, R.James Bender Publishing Co., San Jose CA, USA (1985)

Buchner, Alex, *Der Bergkrieg im Kaukasus: Die Gebirgstruppe 1942*, Podzun-Pallas-Verlag, Freidberg, Germany (1977)

Davis, Brian L., *German Army Uniforms and Insignia 1933-1945*, Arms & Armour Press Ltd., London, UK (1971)

Fowler, E.W.W., *Nazi Regalia*, Bison Books Ltd., London, UK (1992)

Lee, Cyrus A., *Soldat: The World War II German Army Collector's Handbook*, 2 vols., Pictorial Histories Publishing Co., Montana, USA (1988 & 1991)

McGuirk, Dal, *Rommel's Army in Africa*, Century Hutchinson Australia Pty.Ltd., Melbourne, Australia (1987)

Mollo, Andrew, *German Uniforms of World War II*, Macdonald & Janes Ltd., London, UK (1976)

Peterson, Daniel, *Wehrmacht Camouflage Uniforms & Post-War Derivatives*, EM17, Windrow & Greene Ltd., London, UK (1995)

Pruett, Michael H., & Edwards, Robert J., *Field Uniforms of German Army Panzer Forces in World War II*, J.J.Fedorowicz Publishing Inc., Winnipeg, Canada (1993)

Rottman, Gordon L., *German Combat Equipments 1939-1945*, MAA 234, Osprey Publishing Ltd., London, UK (1991)

Stewart, Emilie, *A Collector's Guide to World War II Wehrpasses and Soldbuchs*, privately published, Ohio, USA (1985)

Williamson, Gordon, *German Military Police Units 1939-1945*, MAA 213, Osprey Publishing Ltd., London, UK (1989)

Windrow, Martin, *The Panzer Divisions*, MAA 24 (Revised Edn.), Osprey Publishing Ltd., London, UK (1982)

Winter, Robert E., *Chain Dogs: The German Army Police in World War II*, Pictorial Histories Publishing Co., Montana, USA (1994)

Periodicals:
Militaria Magazine (French language edition), Histoire & Collections, Paris, France
Militaria Magazine (English language edition), Collectors Press Ltd., London, UK
Military Illustrated Past & Present, Military Illustrated Ltd., London, UK